From The Library Of
REV. RICHARD E. PLYLER

HOW TO BECOME
SUPER-
SPIRITUAL
or Kill Yourself Trying

HOW TO BECOME
SUPER-
SPIRITUAL
or Kill Yourself Trying

John Sterner

Abingdon
Nashville

HOW TO BECOME SUPER-SPIRITUAL
OR KILL YOURSELF TRYING

Copyright © 1982 by Abingdon

Library of Congress Cataloging in Publication Data

STERNER, JOHN, 1942–
How to become super-spiritual or kill yourself trying.
1. Christian life—1960– . I. Title.
BV4501.2.S756   248.4   82-6636   AACR2

ISBN 0-687-17760-X

"Listen to the Mustn'ts" is from *Where the Sidewalk Ends* by Shel Silverstein (text only) copyright © 1974 by Shel Silverstein. Reprinted by permission of Harper & Row, Publishers, Inc. The lines from *Knots* by R. D. Laing are copyright © 1970 by the R. D. Laing Trust. Reprinted by permission of Pantheon Books, a division of Random House, Inc. The lines on page 114 are from *You're in Charge* by Cecil Osborne copyright © 1973 by Word Incorporated, page 128. Used by permission of Word Books, Publisher, Waco, Texas 76796. The lyrics on page 117 are from "Jolly Old Sigmund Freud," in the *Anna Russell Song Book*. Copyright © 1960 by Anna Russell. Published by arrangement with Lyle Stuart.

Scripture passages noted NEB are from The New English Bible; those noted Phillips are from The New Testament in Modern English, Rev. Ed., by J. B. Phillips; those noted NIV are from The Holy Bible: New International Version; those noted JB are from The Old Testament of The Jerusalem Bible; those noted TLB are from *The Living Bible;* those noted NAB are from The New American Bible; those noted TEV are from the Good News Bible: The Bible in Today's English Version; those noted NAS are from the New American Standard Bible; those noted RSV are from the Revised Standard Version of the Bible; those noted Goodspeed are from The Complete Bible, an American Translation, by J. M. Powis Smith and Edgar J. Goodspeed; all others are from the King James Version.

MANUFACTURED BY THE PARTHENON PRESS AT
NASHVILLE, TENNESSEE, UNITED STATES OF AMERICA

C O N T E N T S

AUTHOR'S   BACKWORD

I feel like a fugitive from the law of averages.
                                    —*Bill Maulden*

I am writing a Backword for two reasons. First, I finished this book before I started it. Second, in the view of most people, I have always marched to the beat of a very different drummer.

A quick observation of my report cards would reveal that teacher remarks fell into two categories: "Does not work up to his potential" and "Poor attitude." (I always wondered just how they knew the potential was there, since I never had worked up to it.) As I told my high school class's twentieth reunion not long ago, "I was the unofficial class agnostic, so of course I became a minister. I was always considered a bit crazy, so I became a psychologist." And now here is my first book, written by a D student in Senior English.

The question that got me into trouble then—Why?—is the same one that gets me into hot water now. I am too psychological for my minister friends and too religious for most psychologists. Because of my views and procedures, I have been fired or asked to resign from five

7

religious organizations (sometimes for being too liberal; sometimes for being too conservative).

So here is a book about Why.

I want to dedicate this book to Stan Voth, Ward Williams, J. Harold Ellens, and my wife Cheryl—four friends who have inspired me by absolutely refusing to be anybody but themselves. I want to thank Nancy Higgerson for correcting my lousy spelling and punctuation, and Debby Osborne for the final typing of the mess given to her.

LISTEN TO
THE MUSTN'TS

Listen to the MUSTN'TS, child
Listen to the DON'TS
Listen to the SHOULDN'TS
The IMPOSSIBLES, the WON'TS
Listen to the NEVER HAVES
Then listen close to me—
Anything can happen, child,
ANYTHING can be.

—Shel Silverstein,
Where the Sidewalk Ends

C H A P T E R 1

The Game

Its name is Public Opinion. It is held in reverence. It settles everything. Some think it is the voice of God.

—Mark Twain

Clara Churchmouse sits obediently in the folding chair. "We really must remember to give our full attention to the situation of the declining revenue of . . . " As the chairperson drones on, Clara's mind begins to wander. "Just how many of these meetings have I been to? How many more do I have to go to? Why is each one just like the last one?"

Her back begins to ache (not to mention her backside) and she resolves, "I just will *not* come to one of these silly meetings again. Not ever! No matter *what* they think, I simply will not endure this any more."

But the next month Clara is back again, in the same folding chair, with the same ache, telling herself the same thing. Next year she will accept the nomination for vice-president of the group she despises. Why?

Ralph Righteous corners an acquaintance at work. "Just started the new wing on the Sunday school building, Charlie. Don't hardly have space enough to hold 'em no more. Gonna cost a bundle, but ya can't stop the work of the Lord. By the way, Charlie, what are you running over at First Church?"

Ralph knows that First Church has not been doing too well for some time. Why is he putting Charlie down?

In his study, Pastor Plushwell is hard at work on the morning message. He gathers quotes from *Time* magazine, scans the newspaper, then arranges references from the Bible (King James Version, "like Paul used") to back up his opinions on the "terrible goin's on today."

A typical Plushwell sermon will blast the National Council of Churches, college students, liberals (*liberal* is defined as anyone who disagrees with Plushwell), and most of the other churches in town. The government is frequently described as "full of liberal commies," and the faithful are continually warned against associating with people who have different theological or political views from those of the pastor.

Pastor Plushwell has a large and growing church, a beautiful home, a wife who avoids him, and an ulcer. Why?

Same Song— Different Words

Clara, Ralph, and the Reverend Plushwell are all doing the same thing. They may appear different and say different words, but they all are pursuing the same goal. They are trying to be super-spiritual, and they are killing themselves in the process.

R. D. Laing, in his book *Knots,* describes Clara, Ralph, and the pastor beautifully.

> They are playing a game.
> They are playing at not playing a game.

> If I show them I see they are, I shall break the rules
> and they will punish me.
> I must play their game of not seeing that I see the game.

If accused of being super-spiritual, our three friends would deny angrily that they were trying to be anything. "I'm just working for the Lord," they would cry.

Spiritual
Versus
Super-Spiritual

Two thousand years ago, Jesus said, "I will build my church; and the gates of hell shall not prevail against it" (Matt. 16:18). The church *did* storm hell time after time in those early years, so that the "Lord added to the church daily" (Acts 2:47). The early Christians were described by their enemies as people who "turned the world upside down" (Acts 17:6 RSV).

Today, some critics of Christianity describe the work of our Lord as being something quite different from the Christianity of Galilee. They say that the church has become "fossilized." In two thousand years, it has regressed from a dynamic force to a decaying fossil. How? By trying to become super-spiritual.

What Does
Super-Spiritual
Mean?

Just what do I mean by *super-spiritual?* According to Webster, *super* means *a higher rank or position. Spiritual* means *of the Spirit.* So, for our purposes, the word *super-spiritual* means *a higher rank or position in the realm of the Holy Spirit.* It means that one has arrived at a place of honor and implies that one has more spiritual fruit and is closer to God than before becoming super-spiritual. It

13

usually also suggests that one is more pious than others not so super-spiritually inclined.

"Well, what's so bad about that?" you might ask. "Aren't we *supposed* to grow in Christ and become more spiritual?" Yes! Absolutely and unequivocally, *yes!* But there is a great deal of difference between becoming more spiritual and being super-spiritual.

To become more spiritual is the goal of every sincere child of God. It is a day-by-day, week-by-week adventure in the kingdom of God. It involves discipline, patience, and training. It requires a sincere faith in and love for the Lord Jesus Christ. It is described by Paul as pressing on "toward the mark for the prize of the high calling of God in Christ Jesus" (Phil. 3:14). Its rewards are the spiritual fruit of love, joy, and peace (Gal. 5:22).

Everybody Wants to Be Somebody— Nobody Wants to Grow

Spiritual growth is hard work. We try, fail, get up and try again. We succeed a bit, fall on our faces, get up, and go on. The ultimate victory over sin, self, and Satan is guaranteed by our Lord. "In the world ye shall have tribulation: but be of good cheer; I have overcome the world" (John 16:33b). The battles, however, are tough— tough enough to make a sincere child of God wish for an easier way. And Satan is right on the spot with what looks for all the world like a divine answer.

Satan comes to us as a sincere, logical angel of light, with the message, "You don't have to fight; why work so hard? Just be like *this*, believe *that*, have these spiritual experiences, follow that man or doctrine or denomination. Then you've got it made."

Super-spirituality is Satan's shortcut to real spirituality. It usually involves being "like" someone or something else. It is copping out to man's rules

14

concerning religion. It is trying to reach the goals God has set for you, using the ways of man. Jesus says that anyone who does this is a thief and a robber (John 9:1). Super-spirituality is Phariseeism, legalism, death. When the person involved finds that the way is not producing real spirituality, he or she pretends spirituality. Thus *super-spirituality actually prevents a person from becoming more spiritual.* How this happens will be seen in the following chapters.

Together, we will look at several types of super-spirituality. Some types will make you laugh. Have a good time! Some will make you cry, and that's OK, too. Some will make you angry. When this happens, it usually will be because you have been caught by what I have said. You are invited to repent of this type of super-spirituality.

Everyone I know (including myself) is a hypocrite. If that sounds harsh, consider yourself, your church, your close friends. Do you know anyone who *never* pretends to have his or her life a little more together than it really is?

CHAPTER 2

Work, Work, Work!

Super-Spiritual Labor

A committee is a group of the unprepared, appointed by the unwilling, to do the unnecessary. —Fred Allen

There probably is no organization in the world (with the possible exception of government) that can produce as many committees which do little or nothing as can the church. This fact is especially hard for me to live with because the church is supposed to be engaged in the most important business in the world: teaching humankind how to live, now and forever.

At a church where I once worked, my schedule was never without a meeting of one kind or another. Sometimes I went to three or four meetings in a single day. I described myself as "busy in the work of the Lord," and I was very proud of myself for working so hard.

Those of us who were on all those committees (ever notice that it's always the same people?) used to complain a lot about our busy schedules, our hard work, the fact that we never had time for ourselves or our families and that some of the others ought to carry their share of the load.

Such a Way
to Run a Business

It was during one of those pity parties (isn't it fun to be ill-used?) that one committee member shocked me by saying, "Well, why do we have all these useless meetings in the first place? Why, if I ran my business the way we run this church, I'd go broke in a week!"

At first, I told myself (and him) that he just did not understand the Lord's work. But his words began to haunt me like Marley's ghost. I began to actually listen to the words being said at our meetings. As I listened, I began to think heretical thoughts: Why am I here at this meeting? What is its function, besides meeting each month and reading the minutes of the last meeting? Is this really the Lord's work? Or is it the work of the church, for that matter?

The problem with the church system is that nothing ever has been allowed to die its natural death. We see a need, plan a method to meet that need, and implement the plan. The plan then becomes a part of the system. Years go by, and the need no longer exists, but we still try to keep the plan going because it is now part of the system.

Two hundred years ago, Robert Raikes saw an opportunity to teach children to read and thus to study the Word of God. He made a plan. His plan was called the Sunday school. Despite the inevitable opposition, he put his plan into action. (Anyone with a new idea is a crank until the idea works.) Today, no self-respecting church is without a building full of classrooms, blackboards, and books. These very expensive buildings, though generally used only once a week, nevertheless take up a large portion of the churches' time, money, and talent.

Jesus said, "Heaven and earth shall pass away: but my words shall not pass away" (Mark 13:31). I do not think that Jesus would spend much time in the average church committee meeting. I think he would say, "Why in the

17

world are you working so hard to keep that thing going? It is a part of the heaven and earth that will pass away."

The feeble excuse that we've "always done it that way" is simply not true. Once, we got along without the Sunday school. There may come a time when we no longer will need it. We always will need to teach God's Word, but not necessarily in a big building on Sunday morning at 10:00.

Beige Draperies

Another popular fallacy is that committees accomplish a lot of work. In reality, there is something about a group of people that makes me want to show off my wisdom and knowledge. I suspect that others have this problem also, since it seems to take a great deal of time for a group to do what one person could have done very quickly. The common answer to this is that better decisions are made by groups of people, because their wisdom is pooled. But what if they are not wise? It has been my experience that in most committees, one or two people make the decisions, and the others go along with them.

The chancellor of a university in California explained the reason that his lovely house on campus has beige draperies and rugs. "The house was decorated by a committee," he said, "and beige is the only shade any committee can agree upon." GOD SO LOVED THE WORLD THAT HE DIDN'T SEND A COMMITTEE, states a sign.

Death of a Meeting

Last year I was involved in the local ministerial association. We had monthly meetings which were attended by about 10 percent of the ministers in the county. We tried everything we knew to boost attendance. We planned what we thought were exciting meetings, sent invitations, and made phone calls, only to have the same faithful few each month. We tried devotionals, guest speakers, coffee and doughnuts. Nothing worked. Finally at one of the meetings, we got down to the root of the problem. Why were we there, anyway?

Our speaker had brought a taped message about small-group sharing for ministers. He called these organizations *support groups.* I remember only one sentence. "Why," said the speaker, "should the pastor be the loneliest man in town?" After we heard the tape, we began to reveal to one another the real reason we came each month. We came because we were lonely and wanted fellowship. "I really need a group where I can just be *me* and not 'the pastor,'" said one. "Me too," said another. "I want a group that will listen to me and understand." The Amens went around the room.

"Then why do we bother with agenda, elections, minutes, and programs, if all we want to do is have fellowship?" asked a heretic. The result was to effectively kill off the association as we knew it, and we began to meet *twice* a month from 7:00 to 9:00 in the morning for coffee, fellowship, and prayer. We call it The Group, and we have more people coming now than we did for the old meetings.

Look closely at the different groups in your church. Ask yourself, What need does each one serve? Is it *necessary* to have regular meetings, or could it meet only when needed? Can it be eliminated entirely? Could it be merged with another group? Could the job be done better by one or two people?

"Okay, okay," you say, "but I don't waste my time in groups that have no meaning. I spend my time winning souls for the Lord, going to prayer meetings, and reading the Bible. I'm *really* busy in the Lord's work, right?" Maybe. And maybe not. The question is not, Is this the Lord's work? (My spiritual grandmother used to say that the Lord would do his *own* work.) The question for me is, Is this *my* work? Is this what God wants *me* to do?

Work Is a Copout?

Let's face it, there are times when our wonderful kids are not so wonderful, our sweet wife is not too sweet, our kind husband is not so kind, and our happy home is not very happy. BE REASONABLE; DO IT MY WAY, I have seen on posters. In my home there are six very different personalities with six different plans for doing things, and each wants the other five to "be reasonable." There are many ways of dealing with conflict, and one way is to avoid dealing with it all, to escape.

Some people escape into alcohol and/or drugs, but for me to do this would result in my being fired. Escape into a mental institution does not appeal to me. But there is one escape that is approved by my church, my superiors, and the rest of society—work. After all, I am busy for the Lord. And he comes first, right? It is so easy to "get busy" when there are conflicts at home. This is Pastor Plushwell's problem and the probable cause of his negative preaching. (It is also the probable cause of his ulcer, for "hope deferred maketh the heart sick" [Prov. 13:12].)

Working? —Or Living?

Super-spirituality says, "Busy is good; busy-busy is even better!" Some are so busy in the "work of the Lord" that they never do the work the Lord really has given them to do. I try to keep my priorities straight in this manner: My personal spiritual growth (prayer, Bible study, books) comes first, because I know that I will live with God forever and that I will live with *myself* forever.

My relationship with my wife comes second, because I intend to live with her for a long time, too. My children are third, because God has made me responsible for them until they leave home. *Then* come my pastoral responsibilities, because I simply will not be with my congregation as long as I will be with God, my wife, or my children.

What does this mean in practical living? It means that last week I skipped a prayer meeting to take my son to a football game. It means that last year I turned down a funeral to take my wife on a vacation. It means that I bought a telephone-answering system in order to have an uninterrupted dinner and devotional time with my family. It means that when I preach that Christianity begins at home, people believe me (although not all of them agree with me). It means that if another church hires me, they had better be prepared to be in fourth place.

In my counseling practice, I see many Clara Churchmice. Their families are neglected; they are always tired and depressed, always in a constant state of flurry, hurry, and worry. Most of them are doing church work to convince themselves that they are worthwhile people. Clara Churchmouse and Pastor Plushwell do not really like themselves, and in their hearts, they are convinced that God really does not like them either. So they work. They work to prove to God and to other church members, but mostly to themselves, that they are acceptable persons, worth something to God. And it does not really matter if anything is *accomplished*, as long as they stay busy.

"Martha, Martha, you are fretting and fussing about so many things; but one thing is necessary." We are so distracted by our many tasks that we forget to sit at the feet of Jesus. "The part that Mary has chosen is best; and it shall not be taken away from her" (Luke 10:41-42 NEB). A friend of mine used to say, "You know, God's a lonely

21

guy. Everybody's out doing his work, and no one takes time to talk to him about it."

Clara and Pastor Plushwell, the Lord loves both of you. Not your works, not your righteousness (really filthy rags) but *you*—plain sinful old you. If you would drop some of your excess baggage, put your own houses in order, and learn to be Christlike with your spouses and children (who bitterly resent your work, work, work), you both might just find the joy of your salvation. If you insist on being like Martha, you will complain like she did. Why not choose to be like Mary and learn to live like she did?

There is one danger for you, though, Clara: Your Martha friends will not understand. Those you have served with for years, spinning your wheels, will think you have backslidden, fallen from grace, or at least are out of fellowship with the Lord. They will continue to play their super-spiritual game and resent the fact that you no longer play it with them—especially if you seem perfectly happy about it; *most* especially is your family is happy about it; and most *certainly* especially if you become closer to God as a direct result. (One thing super-spirituality cannot stand is *real* spirituality.)

Be prepared, Pastor, the way is rough. "All that will live godly in Christ Jesus shall suffer persecution" (II Tim. 3:12). The rewards, however, are far greater than the persecution. Good luck, Pastor, and hang in there!

C H A P T E R 3

Look at Me!

Super-Spiritual Success

*When people are free to do as they please, they usually imitate
each other.* —*Eric Hoffer*

In a small pentecostal inner-city church, an offering is
being taken. "I want twenty people to take out a $20 bill
and put it on the altar, and God will bless you," says the
preacher. "Let us pray."

During the prayer, two persons respond to the plea.
But just then, from the choir, comes a word of prophecy.
"Thus saith the Lord God of hosts: Yea and I say to the
other eighteen, get thee down and give; do not disobey
my voice as your fathers did in the wilderness and saw
my wrath, but get thee down and give, and I will surely
bless thee." Sure enough, eighteen more of the faithful
got them down and gave, obeying the voice of God. (This
is a true story, witnessed by a fellow minister.)

I regularly receive invitations to seminars which
propose to teach me how to develop a "successful
church" (one with lots of people and money). Those
extending the invitations have slogans: Fastest Growing
Church in the Universe, or Capturing the Whole Country
for Christ. One invitation aims to show me how the
congregation can grow from seventy-six to two thousand

in a few years. I regularly throw these invitations in the trash can.

What do the "successful church" invitations have in common with the inner-city church? Both are different versions of the super-spiritual show-off.

Ornaments
on a Dead Tree

I happen to pastor in a denomination that believes in the practice of the spiritual gifts mentioned in First Corinthians 12. I regularly practice, and I encourage others to practice those gifts. I am happy when our worship is blessed by the gifts, and I pray that we might be blessed even more. (I *do* want my district superintendent to know that I am not a heretic.)

What bothers me, though, in our denomination and in others like it, and among the charismatics in other churches, is a "look at me" attitude when it comes to spiritual gifts. "Bless God, I've got it!" (With the unspoken questions: Why don't *you* have it? Don't you wish you did?)

We seem to delight in parading our gifts, forgetting the God who gave them to us. I have heard people compare their spiritual experiences. "Last week I had a vision of God" (have *you* ever had one?); "I'll never forget my baptism in the Holy Ghost" (*my* baptism? I thought *Jesus* gave it to you). Those without similar experiences are properly awed and put down. They are made to feel like second-class citizens of the kingdom of God, and they worry about not having what the others have.

The show-off forgets three things. First, that *God* gave the gifts. "Every good . . . and . . . perfect gift is from above, and cometh down from the Father" (James 1:17). Second, that we do not need to be good or spiritual or righteous or deserving to receive gifts. To receive gifts, we simply need to "ask, and it shall be given" (Matt. 7:7).

24

Third, that a father gives different gifts to different children, according to their needs and the results he wants to accomplish in their lives.

Take, for instance, an evergreen tree. There it sits in the middle of the forest, doing its thing. One day a woodchopper comes along, cuts the tree down, and puts it on a truck. The tree is placed on a lot, bought, taken to a home, and finally decorated.

Suppose that the tree, looking down at the twinkling lights, the gaily colored ornaments, the shining tinsel, says to itself, "Look at me! I'm really something!" Wouldn't that be ridiculous? Wouldn't we say to the tree, "You fool! You did not decorate yourself. Those gifts were placed upon you for a purpose, and when there is no need for them they will be removed by those who put them there." (As a matter of fact, as the tree begins to die, the gifts look out of place.)

Pride
Is the Problem

We can stop being proud of our spiritual gifts, because we ourselves did not produce them; they were given to us. Instead, we can learn to use them for the glory of God and for the building up of his Church. If we continue to boast about them, we will become like the dead tree with the pretty ornaments—strange looking, out of place, super-spiritual.

Pride in our gifts will lead to our destruction (Prov. 16:18). We will begin to use our gifts to manipulate the wills of others, rather than permitting God to manifest his power by blessing others through us. One passage of Scripture to keep in mind when considering the use and abuse of gifts is First Corinthians 12:7, "The manifestation of the Spirit is given to every man to profit withal." Or, as J. B. Phillips puts it, "The Spirit openly makes his gift to each man, so that he may use it for the common good."

Do you use *your* gift, your talents, your abilities to build up others? Is the common good of the saints increased when you minister (serve others) with your gift? If we cannot say yes to these questions, we are in danger of becoming followers of Balaam.

The Immoral
Prophet

The story of Balaam is a perfect example of God's gifts being in an unclean vessel. Hired by Balak, king of Moab, to curse the Israelites, Balaam blesses them instead. "I paid you to curse these people," cries Balak. "Why are you blessing them?" In his answer, Balaam gives a prophecy so beautiful that we sing it in the church today. "God is not a man, that he should lie; neither the son of man, that he should repent: hath he said, and shall he not do it? or hath he spoken, and shall he not make it good?" (Num. 23:19).

After giving these wonderful and true prophecies, Balaam advises the king to persuade Israel to commit sexual sin and idol worship. Balaam is later killed by the avenging Israelite army and his name becomes of great reproach to the Jews; in Second Peter 2:15, he is referred to as a lover of unrighteousness.

The point is that God does not judge our spirituality by gifts, but by fruit. God is responsible for giving gifts. It is our responsibility to walk in the Spirit, abide in the vine, and grow the fruits of love, joy, and peace found in Galatians 5:22, 23.

Bigger
Is Better?

Now, I am willing to admit to a good deal of green-eyed monster when I think about the big churches with buses, choir robes, radio programs, and large full-time staffs. Why am I bothered? Because I want a big deal, too.

Part of the reason I am so turned off, though, is because of the never-ending bragging in the invitations. "Be like us!" they shout, implying that not only is it possible to be like them, but it is desirable and even necessary to be like them.

Americans are constantly looking for the biggest, the fastest, the most expensive—the record breaker. One of my son's favorite books is the *Guinness Book of World Records*. We eat dinner in a restaurant that has served X million hamburgers. We brag that our denomination is the fastest growing in the world and that our Sunday school has more members than somebody else's.

On the other hand, Jesus avoided crowds. He even preached a sermon (John 6) that diminished his following from more than five thousand down to twelve. "From that time many of his disciples went back, and walked no more with him" (v. 66). I wonder if they teach *that* kind of preaching in those classes?

Once, our bus minister (we have one bus) and I became extremely excited after attending one of those seminars. We bought books, tape recordings, information, and graphics—all designed to enable us to grow, like another church in our denomination. We read the directions, we plotted, we planned, we prayed, we copied the methods of churches that had been small and had grown large.

For one month, we gave away balloons, bubble gum, and transistor radios. We had Sardine Sunday, Halloween Mask Sunday and Pastor's Pizza Party Sunday. We used professional materials supplied by the seminar. We visited, canvassed, exhorted, and we bombed out. Our attendance was actually less than usual during the big push. We dropped the program.

Be Yourself

As I look back on that experience, I think the Lord was telling us that it is not nearly as important to become big, as to be faithful to his purpose for us. God does not care whether our church is like any other church. We have a special ministry in our town—one that no other church can fulfill. To focus upon the ministry of another church and try to be like it is to be super-spiritual. To become *really* spiritual, we must focus upon the ministry God gives to us.

Bill Gothard is fond of saying that we are responsible for the depth of our message, but that God is responsible for its breadth. The bus experience set me free to become more like the minister that God had intended me to be when he saved me. I discovered that God never had intended me to be like Billy Graham. He already *had* one of those. God wants me to be *me*. Just me. For me to try to be like Dr. Graham would be super-spiritual. To be really spiritual, I only need to become the best me that I can be (and nobody else can be *that* but me).

What are you proud of? Your brand new building? Your spiritual gift? Your salvation? The fact that you belong to a "Bible-believing, fundamental, gospel-preaching" church? The healing that God gave you? That you have been blessed financially? That you can sing, preach, or write books? What do you have that God did not give you? Praise God for it, but *please* try not to be proud of it.

Your attitude should be the same as that of Christ Jesus:

> Who, being in very nature God,
> > did not consider equality with God something
> > > to be grasped,
> but made himself nothing,
> > taking the very nature of a servant,
> > being made in human likeness.
> And being found in appearance as a man,
> > he humbled himself
> > and became obedient to death—
> > > even death on a cross!

Therefore God exalted him to the highest place
  and gave him the name that is above every name,
that at the name of Jesus every knee should bow,
  in heaven and on earth and under the earth,
and every tongue confess that Jesus Christ is Lord,
  to the glory of God the Father. (Philippians 2:5-11 NIV)

The Super-Spiritual Reverse

It also is quite possible to be proud of *not* being large or of *not* having gifts or of *not* numbering important people among the congregation. This is called the super-spiritual reverse, or the 'ole humble bit. "Bless God, we're small, but we're spiritual." I do *not* think that big is bad, or that small is good, but that *you* are *you*.

What are you ashamed of? Is your building old and run down? Or do you think you need something that someone else or some other church has? Take heart; God loves you just the way you are. "What proves that God loves us is that Christ died for us while we were still sinners" (Rom. 5:8 JB).

Warning 1

Super-spiritual people cannot stand people who are just being themselves. You will be encouraged, exhorted, prayed for, and preached at to become "like the rest of us." In fact, if you become too happy about being yourself, you may be given the left foot of fellowship.

Warning 2

There is great danger, once you have been set free from being like everyone else, that you will become proud of it—proud of being free. Resist the temptation to tell everyone in your church how wonderful it is to be free (and that *they* should become free like *you* are). Let them see your light shining in their darkness! Let them feel your love, your joy, your peace in knowing that you no

29

longer must strive to be like the others. Let them ask you about it.

Warning 3

Finally, remember to repent when you blow your humility. Whenever you catch yourself trying to be like someone else, change your mind and say, "God, what would you have me be?" And by the way, try not to be too proud of being so humble.

Joybells

Super-Spiritual Solemnity

Joy is about as rare as the bald eagle. —*Vernon Grounds*

On a recent Sunday evening, our song leader looked at the faces in the congregation and remarked, "You people look like Pontius Pilate at a Christmas party." I looked around. Where was the joy of the Lord in which lies our strength? We looked so unhappy being there; why were we there at all?

Observe the faces at your next worship service. Do they look happy to be there in their pews? Does each face say, "Boy, I can hardly wait to see what the Lord will do"? Or does it say, "Boy, I can hardly wait to get out of here and watch the game"? Are they glad to be in the house of the Lord? Or are they doing their duty, fulfilling their religious obligation?

The psalmist tells us that we are to "enter into his gates with thanksgiving, and into his courts with praise: be thankful unto him, and bless his name" (Ps. 100:4). Why is there such a great difference between the spirit of the psalms and the spirit of our churches? We are so glum that the philosopher Nietzsche commented, "I would believe in their salvation, if they looked a little more like people who have been saved." How has the salt of the earth become so tasteless?

One reason for our lack of joy is that we do not realize where joy originates. Vernon Grounds puts it this way:

Consider first the source of genuine joy. God, Paul declares, is the blessed and only Pontentate (I Tim. 6:15). Since blessed means happy, Paul is here speaking of the happy God. If all truth and beauty and goodness are rooted in the very nature of our Creator, so too is all joy. *God is not a grim and emotionless tyrant.* . . . God is the source of all genuine joy. ("Soar with the Eagle," *Christianity Today* 20 [August 27, 1976], italics added)

Did you know that God laughs? (Ps. 2:4); that he rejoices over his people with singing and joy? (Zeph. 3:17); that joy is an angelic emotion? (Luke 15:10). "So go ahead, eat, drink, and be merry," says Solomon. "Wear fine clothes—with a dash of cologne! Live happily with the woman you love through the fleeting days of life, for the wife God gives you is your best reward down here for all your earthly toil" (Eccl. 9:7-9 TLB).

Somewhere, somehow, Satan has convinced the church that joy comes from pleasure, which comes from the world, which is controlled by Satan. Therefore joy must be satanic, and we had jolly well better be solemn (*solemn*, by the way, is defined by Webster as *sacred, serious, impressive* and does *not* mean a lack of joy).

Don't Be Worldly

We have been taught to overemphasize the sinfulness of the world. "Wherefore come out from among them, and be ye separate," seems to be our favorite line (II Cor. 6:17). We are constantly warned against becoming "worldly," which means whatever the person who says it *wants* it to mean. Evangelist David Wilkerson tells that when he was a boy, the "mark of the beast" was interpreted as being the choir robes of the "worldly" churches.

This pessimistic view teaches church members to be

constantly on their guard lest Satan soil them with the sins of the world. If one asks them what their church believes, one will hear a long list of things they *cannot* do. If one asks them *why* they cannot do them, they will say, "Because our church doesn't believe in it."

No Fun

These people are seldom fun to be with. Their favorite sermons center around the Last Days, when Jesus will pay back all those terrible worldly people with fire, darkness, wailing, and gnashing of teeth. They love to hear about the sinfulness of the world, the threat of communist takeovers in our colleges, and the "worldliness" of the churches who disagree with them. Their God is pictured as a grumpy old man in the sky, with a clipboard, looking angrily about and writing down the names of anyone having fun.

Now lest I be misunderstood, I believe in the total fall of humankind, that the world system is controlled by Satan, and that Christ will return soon to judge all people. I also believe that as a Christian, I should live differently from those whose lives are controlled by sin. But I happen to believe that, because I am a new creature in Christ, my joy in serving my Lord should be so great that I will separate myself from sin *willingly*.

Recently, one of my youngsters was asked which church her daddy pastors. When she told her friends, they said, "Oh, that's the one where you can't smoke or drink or dance." While they are small, my children will separate themselves from sin because I tell them to. But if they do not learn a good reason for the rules, they will drop them when they are older. It will never work to just say, "Because our church doesn't believe in it."

God Owns the World

"The earth is the Lord's, and the fulness thereof; the world, and *they that dwell therein*" (Ps. 24:1, italics

33

added). God created the world and gave dominion over it to humankind (Gen. 1:28). Humankind sold its birthright to Satan in the Garden, and God bought it back on the cross. While the majority of the people in the world still belong to Satan, those of us who are saved are now owned by God. "Ye are bought with a price; be not ye the servants of men" (I Cor. 7:23). Those pleasures that give me joy are given to me by God. Satan may try to twist them and pervert them to corrupt me, but if I walk in the Spirit, I am promised joy, love, peace, and the assurance that I will not fulfill the lust of the flesh.

Let the world pervert the pleasures of God. Let others run after gurus, sexual immorality, drugs, suicide, and snowmobiles, chasing joy, love, and peace. I am living in the kingdom of God. And in that Kingdom there is joy in serving Jesus. "The trouble with most people," says Bob Harrington, "is that they've got just enough religion to bug 'em and not enough to bless 'em."

Down with Dignity

Another reason for the doom and gloom on Sunday morning is that we feel we must be dignified in the Lord's house. For heaven's sake, why? Why must we be so different when we are in church than we are in school or at work or at home? "Folly is set in great dignity," says Solomon (Eccl. 10:6), and it is my opinion that we make fools of ourselves on Sunday by trying to be what we are not.

One of my favorite stories in the Bible is that in which David escorted the ark of God to Jerusalem (II Sam. 6). Evidently David was not completely clothed as he "danced before the Lord with all his might" (v. 14). Michal, his wife, saw him dancing and "despised him in her heart." She met him at the door and said, "Boy, did *you* look like a king today. Out there in front of God and all those people, dancing and exposing yourself like some kind of nut" (Sterner Version).

David simply said, "It was before the Lord" (v. 21). And Michal had no children (this was thought to be a curse from God) till the day she died. David was so full of the joy of the Lord that he forgot that he was supposed to be a dignified king. He was willing to look like a fool in front of his own subjects in order to show God how much he loved him.

Not too long ago, our church conducted a vacation Bible school. I taught a class full of unchurched teenagers. The class was fun, relatively unstructured, and the kids called me John. A few weeks later, one of the students visited our morning worship services. "How come your dad acts so different on Sundays?" she asked my daughter. "He's so dignified." How come, indeed?

Acting
Versus Being

Acting—*there* is the whole problem in a nutshell. We play our parts; say our lines automatically, precisely. Now we sing, now we testify, now we listen to the pastor, soon we can go home and watch TV. "All the world's a stage," said Shakespeare, "And all the men and women merely players:/They have their exits and their entrances;/And one man in his time plays many parts" (*As You Like It,* Act II, sc. 7).

We need to stop *acting* like Christians and start *being* Christians. We must stop acting joyful (we don't fool anybody, anyway) and start *being* joyful. To do that, we must first find out how. I propose that we begin by being ourselves in church, and I do not think that we are naturally very dignified.

It is *not* spiritual to be sad. Jesus was accused of being a drunkard and a glutton. John wrote, "These things have I spoken . . . that your joy might be full" (15:11). Paul described the churches in Macedonia as having an abundance of joy. I know that Jesus said that those who mourn were blessed. I know that he is described as a man of sorrows, acquainted with grief. I know that he wept at the tomb of Lazarus. But Paul tells us to "rejoice with them that do rejoice; and weep with them that weep" (Rom. 12:15). Solomon says that "to every thing, there is a season . . . a time to weep, and a time to laugh" (Eccl. 3:1, 4).

I am not suggesting that we make jokes at funerals, but is the worship service a funeral? Are we not instead involved in a celebration of life—abundant life, eternal life, the "good life"? An old Irish blessing reads, "May the blessed sunlight shine upon you and warm your heart till it glows like a great peat fire, so that the stranger may come and warm himself before it and become your friend."

I propose that the goal of the Christian's life, and the celebration of it on Sunday morning is to declare with the angels, "Fear not: for, behold, I bring you good tidings of great joy, which shall be to all people. For unto you is born this day in the city of David a Saviour, which is Christ the Lord" (Luke 2:10-11).

If you love life, life will love you back.
—*Arthur Rubinstein*

C H A P T E R 5

Put on a Happy Face

Super-Spiritual Joy

The human race is a vast assemblage of individuals who are counterfeiting happiness. —Samuel Johnson

It is 9:00 A.M. on Sunday, at the Smith home. Mary Smith has dragged herself out of bed, made breakfast for the family, dragged the family out of bed to eat the breakfast, and now is trying to get them ready to drag to church.

"Sammy, get your shoes on. No, not those shoes, you dummy, your church shoes! Where are they? How should I know? You better find them, or else! Never mind or else what! . . . Suzy, how on earth do you always manage to get dirty just before church? Change your dress and stop your crying! . . . John, can you put your precious paper down long enough to help a little? Get Sammy's shoes on and put the dog out! Why can't you ever help me on Sunday without being asked?"

The Smiths, late as usual, fight all the way to church, also as usual. But when they arrive, something almost magical happens. John opens the car door, takes Mary's hand, and puts on a big smile. Then they walk into church, where Mary teaches her Sunday school class about love. (The fight resumes after church.)

What is happening here? Super-spiritual joy.

It's Killing Me

The super-spiritual person knows that we are supposed to be joyful in the Lord, because the Bible says so. More important, our pastors and friends say so. To be unhappy is sinful, so if the person is not really happy, he pretends to be. "I will be happy if it kills me," he says. And kill him it does.

While he sings and smiles on the outside, his stomach rebels on the inside. Or he has week-long headaches, for no apparent reason. Or his joints develop arthritis. Doctors are now saying that between 60 and 80 percent of all pain is psychosomatic in origin. This does not mean that our pain is not real or that an ulcer does not actually bleed. It is *not* "all in our head"; it is in whatever parts of our bodies are affected by our heads. We are not imagining these things; in fact, we may well die from them.

The Bible has long been aware of this connection between the mind and the body. "A sound heart is the life of the flesh: but envy the rottenness of the bones" (Prov. 14:30). If we feel good about life, our bodies are less susceptible to disease, according to most psychiatrists. If something or someone hurts us, we can become physically ill. "The words of a talebearer are as wounds, and they go down into the innermost parts of the belly" (Prov. 26:22).

Confessing and Confronting

What does the Bible say we should do about our hurts, our sins, our pain? "Confess your faults one to another, and pray one for another, that ye may be healed" (James 5:16). But what do we actually *do* about our hurts? We hide them. If someone makes a woman angry, she may smile and say, "I'm not upset," while her stomach does gymnastics inside. (She might tell everyone else in the church that she is hurt, but never will she tell the one who hurt her.) "He that covereth his sins shall not prosper:

but whoso confesseth and forsaketh them shall have mercy" (Prov. 28:13).

This "laughing on the outside, crying on the inside" produces what the Bible calls the root of bitterness in our marriages and in our churches. In time, this root of bitterness will grow into a tree of trouble. It will develop fruits of divorce, church splits, and mental breakdowns. It will cause our children to rebel against God and against society. It will ruin our lives.

In chapter eighteen of Matthew, Jesus gave us the formula for taking care of bitterness. If somebody offends me, I am supposed to go right up to him and say, "You offended me." Notice—I go to him *before* I tell my pastor, my wife, or my best friend! Many people have been caught up in bitterness they could have been spared if they had talked to each other instead of to their friends.

If the person who has made me angry will not listen to me, I should go to my pastor or to another spiritual person, and we will go together to talk to the offender. If he will not listen to us, *then* we tell the whole church (not one at a time, but announce it at prayer meeting). I believe that almost all our problems would be solved if we would follow the teaching of Jesus on this matter.

Christians with Problems?

Who originated the idea that salvation gives a person immunity from problems? Paul called himself the chief of sinners and addressed all his letters to churches with problems. Just read his letter to the church at Corinth: sexual problems, arguments, doctrinal disputes, splits in the church, drunkenness, pride. Yet Paul calls the members "sanctified in Christ Jesus, called to be saints." He thanks God for "the grace of God which is given" to them (I Cor. 1:2, 4).

Paul argued with Peter about Jewish tradition and with

Barnabas about correct missionary procedure. John and Charles Wesley did not always see eye to eye. I do not always agree with my board of deacons. People will always disagree, simply because they are people. But Christians are different—not because we do not fight, but because we forgive. Jesus also gave us that procedure in Matthew. Seventy times seven, we are to forgive our brothers—and that's in one day!

I remember my first district council meeting, several years ago. One brother would get up and tell why such-and-such a motion was indispensable to the ongoing movement of the Holy Spirit. As soon as he finished, another brother would get up and explain why the first speaker was all wet. The discussions were long and often hot. But after the matter was voted upon, nobody was angry at anyone else. That is the way the kingdom of God works.

But everyone knows that a person cannot have all those problems and still be super-spiritual. So if you want to rise above all your troubles, just learn one word: Great. Practice it day and night. Great! How's the family? Great! How's the church? Great! How's your migraine? Great! (If you are pentecostal, you can say things like Glory! or Praise the Lord!)

Since your super-spiritual friends do not really want to know how you actually feel anyway, they will be more than satisfied. You will be miserable and lonely inside, but keep thinking about the streets of gold and the mansion over the hilltop, and you will make it "through to the end." Great!

My World
Fell Apart

Several years ago, my whole world collapsed. I was a rising young salesman with a lovely wife, two lovely kids, and a lovely home. Everything was just lovely.

Only it was not, not really. We went to the right church, drove the right car, lived in the right neighborhood, and cultivated the right kind of friends. But we were unhappy.

Rather than dealing with our unhappiness, we went to church more, made more money (and spent more money), and "got involved." We were involved with the choir, the Sunday school, the youth, the mothers, and other groups. But the problems only became worse.

One day I woke up with no job, no wife, no kids. I went to our minister and poured out my heart. "Everybody thinks I'm so happy all the time, because I tell jokes and laugh; but I'm really miserable and lonely, and I'm just a big fake."

He looked at me for a long time and finally said something that blew my mind. "You never really fooled anyone, you know. Just yourself, maybe."

Can you imagine that? Not only were my job, my wife, my kids gone, but my carefully constructed self-image was gone, too! In fact, it never really had existed at all except in my own mind. I was determined that from then on, I would stop pretending to be someone else and just be myself. I have not always succeeded, but I am getting there. (Happily, our family weathered that crisis and was subsequently reunited.)

"Woe to you, teachers of the law and Pharisees, you hypocrites!" (*Hypocrite* is a Greek word, meaning *an actor in a play.*) "You are like whitewashed tombs, which look beautiful on the outside but on the inside are full of dead men's bones and everything unclean. In the same way, on the outside you appear to people as righteous but on the inside you are full of hypocrisy and wickedness" (Matt. 23:27-28 NIV).

What Bothered Jesus?

Did you ever notice how relaxed and unconcerned Jesus seemed to be around persons who were involved in open sin? It was not sin itself that angered him as much as the concealing of sin. (That seemed to bother the American public during the Watergate crisis, too.)

Jesus would sit down and eat with sinners arid publicans. He could easily forgive a woman caught in the act of adultery. But sin covered up by a mask of phony righteousness made him burn. "Ye serpents, ye generation of vipers, how can ye escape the damnation of hell?" (Matt. 23:33).

Jesus knew that sin can be dealt with as long as it is out in the open. "Blessed are those who feel their spiritual need" (Matt. 5:3 Goodspeed). When sin is concealed, hidden from view, it may become hidden even to the sinner. If we pretend long enough, we may eventually believe our pretenses. Repentance and spiritual growth then would be impossible. *"If we confess our sins,* he is faithful and just to forgive us our sins, and to cleanse us from all unrighteousness" (I John 1:9, italics added). We cannot confess our sins and hide them from one another at the same time.

If we hide our sin, pretending joy, real joy will never be ours. "Therefore, if you are offering your gift at the altar and there remember that your brother [or sister, pastor, mother-in-law] has something against you, leave your gift there in front of the altar. First go and be reconciled to your brother; then come and offer your gift" (Matt. 5:23-24 NIV).

It is hard to confess sin. In the short run, it is easier to hide it. But hiding sin makes us miserable. And we know that a Christian is supposed to be happy. And successful. And have his house in order. So—Great! Right? Everything's just great! Only it is not. Unless we are super-spiritual.

The Total Liberated, Submissive, Frustrated Woman

The Super-Spiritual Female

What are little girls made of? —*Traditional Rhyme*

Once upon a time, women knew their "place." It was, as the saying went, in the home. Women did not smoke, drink, vote, or talk back to men. What they *did* do was cook, bake, wash, iron, clean house, sew, mend, garden, and take care of a half dozen or so children. Some authorities say that they were happier then; some say that they were just too tired to protest.

But as another saying goes, times change. Women *did* protest, and they gained more-or-less legal personhood. The *real* change, however, was forced upon them by the industrial revolution. Today machines do the washing, bread comes from stores, other stores carry ready-made clothing that needs no ironing, and day-care centers watch the children. So what is a woman for?

What Is Woman's Role?

Some years ago, researchers at the University of Michigan published a report entitled *Americans View Their Mental Health*. The research team interviewed 2,500 men and women in order to find out how happy Americans considered themselves. Buried in the fourth chapter of

43

the 432-page report is a startling statistic. The team uncovered the fact that most men are satisfied with their marriages, but that the overwhelming majority of women are not!

Why have those women become dissatisfied with their marriages? Because they do not know "who they are"! "The female role in our culture," states the report, "is no longer defined so clearly as the male role. Women in our society are subject to greater stress than men because they don't know what their role really is."

Today you can walk into any Christian bookstore and find a multitude of books that tell women what their role "really is." Some are written by ministers, some by housewives or working women, still others by psychologists. Funny thing, though—all those books claim to be based on the Bible, but they often totally disagree.

Pity the
Poor Housewife

Just how does today's woman fit into the kingdom of God? Here are some who are trying.

Suzy Submissive is totally dedicated to the care and feeding of her husband's ego. Each day of Suzy's life is filled with plans: She plans food that Fred will enjoy, sex that will excite him, and conversation that will be stimulating to him. She plans a fulfilling life—for Fred.

Suzy read somewhere that wives are supposed to submit to their husbands (Eph. 6), and she has been doing it ever since. The trouble is, Suzy is rapidly losing her personality, her friends, and her cool. Her conversation is loaded with "Fred says" and "Fred thinks." Suzy has stopped thinking. She also has stopped going to church because Fred thought she was becoming too religious. She watches only the TV programs Fred likes and has stopped seeing any friends Fred does not care for. She has, for all practical purposes, stopped living.

On the other hand, Lucy Liberated is living it up! She heard in a lecture that there is no difference between male and female, that both are one in Jesus Christ (Gal. 3:28). "So who told him *he* was boss?" she says. "In this family we both wear pants!"

Lucy has a job, an ulcer, and is dangerously close to having a divorce. It is not her job that her husband objects to, although he *says* it is. It is her chip-on-the-shoulder attitude that gets him. Her facial expressions, her tone of voice, her manner fairly scream, "Who do you think you are?" Lucy has liberated herself right into a cage of hostility, bitterness, and separation from her loved ones.

Gloria the Groupie's type was described in chapter 2. Gloria is on four commitees, three bridge clubs, a bowling team, two PTAs, and Cub Scouts, and she rings a bell every Christmas for the Salvation Army. Gloria never argues with her family. This is possible because she never *sees* her family, except in public places.

Dumb Dora is related to Suzy Submissive. Dora is not really dumb—she has an IQ of 128 and received As and Bs in college. But she realizes that her husband, George, is threatened by intelligent women, and so she plays dumb. When someone asks her a question, she always smiles sweetly and says, "Oh, I wouldn't know about that; what do *you* think, George dear?"

Dora's stupidity lies in the fact that she does not realize that she has cheated herself out of an exciting life and that she has cheated George out of an exciting wife. (George is smart, too. He knows what she is doing; he hates himself and soon he will hate her.)

Sally the Super-Mom is described by Erma Bombeck:

Her name was Estelle. I could not believe the inside of her house. The furniture was shining and in place, the mirrors and pictures were hung and there was not a cardboard box in sight. There were fresh flowers on the kitchen table and the books were on the shelves. "You'll have to excuse me," she said, picking a piece of lint off the refrigerator. "Things are such a mess on moving day." *(The Grass Is Always Greener Over the Septic Tank)*

Sally's favorite Bible quotation is "Let all things be done decently and in order" (I Cor. 12:40). Her house is ever-neat, her children are always on the honor role, and she is perpetually smiling. Her husband is seeing another woman—a woman who lets him relax; one who doesn't make him feel like an intruder in his own home.

Bombshell Betty thinks that if she can just keep her husband satisfied sexually, her marital troubles will be over. Betty is wrong. Most men want a lot more from their wives than sex, though it *is* an important part of marriage. Men want to be needed; they want to feel important. They want a good mother for their children, and they appreciate a woman who is a good housekeeper and cook. Most of all, they want a *person*, not just a sex symbol. Men want someone to love them, talk to them, and be their companion for life. Betty never will solve her problems with new manuals for bedroom techniques.

Last of all, there is Velma the Vegetable, who has given up on the whole thing. She has read too many books and become totally confused. Her life now consists of "continuing afternoon dramas" on TV, several boxes of chocolates a day, and about twelve to sixteen hours of sleep. She is constantly depressed and often thinks of suicide. (If you do not believe that female role-confusion can cause this, sit in my office for one day!)

What Is a Woman Worth?

Do you think I overstate my case? I see all these women, from Suzy to Velma, in an average week. Some are depressed, some are filled with anger, most are confused, and most do not like themselves.

In this future-shock society, it is admittedly difficult for women to find identity. Men and women alike have been taught to scorn "women's work" and the women who do it. "I'm just a housewife," is the way my clients put it. *Just* a housewife? Have you ever wondered what a housewife would be earning if she were paid for her work? Here are the facts on the worth of the average homemaker in 1982.

Occupation	Number of Hours Per Week	Rate of Hourly Pay	Total
Nursemaid	44.5	$ 6.08	$270.56
Housekeeper	17.5	8.25	144.38
Cook	13.1	8.25	108.08
Dishwasher	6.2	5.08	31.50
Laundress	5.9	6.37	37.58
Food Buyer	3.3	8.91	29.40
Chauffeur	2.0	8.25	16.50
Maintenance "Man"	1.7	7.64	12.99
Gardener	2.3	7.64	17.57
Seamstress	1.3	8.25	10.72
Dietician	1.2	11.47	13.76
Practical Nurse	0.6	9.55	5.73
Totals	99.6		$698.77

There you are. It adds up to a staggering 99.6-hour work week and a weekly wage of $698.77. Of course, this does not take over-time into consideration, a factor that would skyrocket a homemaker's weekly pay check to $907.09. Add to this her fee as psychiatrist at $75.00 per hour, and you now have some idea of her worth.

"If you can find a truly good wife, she is worth more than precious gems!" says Solomon. "Her husband can trust her, and she will richly satisfy his needs" (Prov. 31:10 TLB). He then goes on to describe how "just a housewife" should be treated. "Her children stand and bless her; so does her husband. . . . There are many fine women in the world, but you are the best of them all!" (Prov. 31:28-29 TLB).

What do women want? The same things men want—to be loved and to feel important. Our lives are largely wrapped up in our work. (That is why so many healthy men and women become ill and die two or three years after retirement.) If my work is unimportant, then *I* also am unimportant. When men discredited the work of women, women soon wanted to do the work of men—the *important* work.

What Are Women Praised For?

When you look at the magazine articles, the TV specials, and the books written about women, you usually will find two things that women are praised for—charm and beauty. Who are the women on the covers of magazines? Who are the guests on the "Tonight Show"? Charming and beautiful women: Brookes, Chers, Lizes. The "beautiful people" get the spotlight. Virtue, kindness, purity of heart, and faithfulness are ignored.

"Charm can be deceptive," continues Solomon, "and beauty doesn't last, but a woman who fears and reverences God shall be greatly praised. Praise her for the many fine things she does. These good deeds of hers shall bring her honor and recognition from even the leaders of the nations" (Prov. 13:30-31 TLB). Any man with seven hundred wives ought to know the worth of a woman!

What is super-spiritual about the women we have examined? Not one of them is being the person God wants her to be. Not one of them is happy. All of them (except Velma) are playing a role that does not fit, in order to reach a goal that does not exist. All of them are so worried about being the kind of wife some book or some other person says a wife should be that they have no idea what *God* wants them to be. And most of them are quoting the Bible to justify their position, just as the books do.

Who's Right?

Now, I am not about to set down rules for women, or for marriage, in this book. But I want you homemakers to know this—that God has designed each woman differently, so that you each can live in a different way and fulfill his plans for this earth. His plan for you may or may not include outside or volunteer work, supremely organized housework, or experiments in bed. You be *you!*

Stop following some set of quasi-biblical rules that worked for someone else. That is the super-spiritual way to disappointment. Find out what *God* wants. Then you can be as liberated, as submissive, or as total as God wants you to be.

C H A P T E R 7

The John Wayne Complex
The Super-Spiritual Male

I'm strong, but I like roses. —*Rod McKuen*

The way I see it, most men need liberation a lot more than women do. Nine out of ten people who come to me for counseling are women. I would like to believe this means that men do not need counseling, but I know better. More men than women commit suicide each year, more men become alcoholics, and more men go to jail. After ten years of Christian work, I am firmly convinced that men have more hang-ups than women *ever* did. So why do they avoid my office as if it were the IRS?

The
Silent Type

The reason most men refuse counseling results from a mind-set that I call the John Wayne Complex. Way back as far as we men can remember, somebody was always telling us to "be a big man." "Big boys don't cry," was the message. "Don't be a baby." Never, under any circumstances, were boys expected to show any emotion other than anger.

Girls were expected to cry when hurt, be afraid of spiders, and hug and kiss their parents. But boys were positively schooled in the art of "It don't bother me." Be strong, be silent, never admit fear, never show joy or pain—never become a person.

What is the result of bringing up a boy under these circumstances? He learns great skill in the neurotic art of denial. Many men do not even cry at the funerals of loved ones. Most men are totally unaware of the tremendous need of their wives and children to be held and cuddled by their husbands or fathers. Some men have no idea that their family wants to hear approving words from them on a regular basis.

Craig Massey, of the Moody Bible Institute, likes to tell about a man he once knew. "I told her that I loved her when we got married," said the man, "and that ought to be enough for her."

I counseled with one family for six months. Most of their problems could have been solved in a few minutes if the father had consented to compliment his wife and children for the things they did right. He stubbornly refused. "After all," he stated, "they're only doing what's right, what's expected of them."

As a result, that man lost his family. Some of his children ran away, some were removed by the court, and his wife filed for divorce. That man was willing to see his entire family dissolve before his eyes, rather than give them a few kind words.

It Only Hurts When I Laugh

Everyone gets hurt sometimes. It is part of living in a world filled with sin. Everyone has experiences that are painful, bitter and that cut deeply. We men bury those experiences deep within our souls. Then we smile

51

through our pain and deny, even to ourselves, that we have been hurt at all.

But like the proverbial bitter pill, those events are hard to swallow. Repressing pain and stress, according to many doctors, can have disastrous results. It causes men, in particular, to suffer strokes, heart attacks, and hardening of the arteries.

The Bible teaches us to "rejoice with them that do rejoice, and weep with them that weep" (Rom. 12:15). There is nothing unmanly about showing deep emotion. Abraham wept at Sarah's death, Jacob wept for Joseph, Jesus wept for Lazarus, and Paul cried "many tears" in the course of his ministry.

On the other hand, Peter tells us to "rejoice with joy unspeakable and full of glory" (I Pet. 1:8).

Men often tell me, "I'm not the emotional type." But they say this with such obvious pride that I doubt that they were born that way. At any rate, there is one emotion they usually have no trouble expressing—anger. Men who never cry or show affection somehow find it easy to become angry, yell, and make everyone either afraid or disgusted. Why is anger the only emotion a man is allowed to express?

The super-spiritual way is to deny all feelings. "There's nothing wrong," we men say through clenched teeth. "I'm just fine." But inside, we know better; we sense a lack of power in the right areas, and we compensate for this lack by seeking to gain power over others—namely, our wives and children.

The Power Play

The secret behind this super-spiritual problem is just that—*power*. Men are trained by our society to be power-grabbers. Look at the programs on TV: Bad guys are being done in violently by the good guys—in the news, in sports, and in the dramas.

We teach our boys to compete for grades, win in sports any way they can (nice guys finish last), and make a "killing" in business. Our school books show Dick running, building, and exploring. Jane happily waits on him hand and foot. Power-grabbing is the name of our game, and woe be unto the boy who shows meekness. *Meekness* rhymes with *weakness*, and weak boys are scorned, left on the sidelines to watch. A girl is censured for fighting. A boy is scolded half-heartedly, then asked, "Did you win?"

Naturally, then, we men cannot afford to show our tears or affections. We certainly must never admit to being afraid. We've got to be strong, *macho*, winners. We must win all our arguments, especially those with our wives and children. WINNING IS NOT THE MOST IMPORTANT THING, reads the poster on the locker room wall. IT'S THE ONLY THING.

Who controls the money in your family? If the wife wants to spend $25 or $50, does she need to ask permission? How about the husband? Couples will talk to me about almost anything—even sex—before they talk about money. Studies show that 75 percent of all marital arguments revolve around money. The real question, though, is not, Who spends the money? but Who has the power?

Dr. Joyce Brothers comments, "When a man treats a woman like a child, he doesn't realize that he may be encouraging her to *act* like a child." I have observed marriages in which the wife was treated like a forty-year-old baby. This is bad for the wife, who becomes depressed and worries about what will happen to her if her husband dies. It is bad for the children, who never learn how to treat a woman. And it is especially bad for the husband, who assumes more responsibility than God ever intended one partner in a marriage to have. No wonder these men develop ulcers and heart attacks!

"Women's Work"?

Most men have a pathological fear of doing "women's work." I know a man who is so caught up in this fear that he refuses to make toast and instant coffee in the morning. If his wife is out, he pouts and goes without, rather than risk being caught doing women's work. Many fathers of large families tell me with pride that they have never changed a diaper in their lives.

Of course, being a professional counselor, I am not caught in those silly hang-ups (I tell myself). *I* wash dishes, diaper babies, and even run an occasional vacuum. But I have an absolute *hostility* toward laundry. Even when my wife was ill for a long period of time, she still folded clothes.

What is there about woman's work that brings out our fears?

More About Power

I think we men view our work as our role in life. Women are looked upon as weak and powerless; therefore women's work is looked upon as making the doer weak and powerless. Many marriages have broken up when the wife began to earn more than the husband. Money equals power, and men want that power to stay in their hands.

Why is it that women can wear pants, tennis shoes, and Army jackets, but men cannot wear skirts, lipstick, or earrings? Power! Women are assuming more power today. They are voting, working outside the home, and taking over a lot of formerly "Men only" positions. They are now literally wearing the pants. Since pants are equated with power, this is OK. If a man were to wear a dress, however, that would be a psychological loss of power, and therefore shameful.

The idea of power is present especially in our sexual

relations. Many psychologists say that our sex life is a microcosm of our total life. In other words, the way a man and a woman relate sexually is usually indicative of the way they treat each other in other areas of their marriage. Many men are threatened, for instance, if the wife initiates sexual activity. This is looked upon as a power play and somehow means that the man must be a weak person.

Neglected Power

Strangely enough, one important area of power often is totally neglected by men. Power over one's self, or temperance, is one fruit of the Holy Spirit listed in Galatians 5:22-23. Solomon praised the man who rules his own spirit and is slow to anger (Prov. 16:32). He said that such a man is greater than a mighty general.

Clearly, God wants his children to maintain mastery over the flesh. Paul compares himself to an athlete who disciplines his body in order to win a race (I Cor. 9:24-27). And here is the strange thing—the man who never shows deep emotion usually is the one who cannot control his will. These men are expending so much emotional energy in controlling their fears, affections, and grief that they lose control over their anger.

"We talk about losing our tempers," says Bob Mumford, "but we always seem to find them again." Have you ever been right in the middle of a temper tantrum, yelling and screaming, when the telephone rang, and some person from your church was on the other end of the line? What did you do? You "found" that lost temper and said sweetly, "Hello, Mrs. Smith, how are you? . . . I'm just fine, thank you."

We know that the spiritual man has control over himself, so we try to control ourselves. But we have been trained to control the wrong areas of our lives. God did

55

not tell us to hide our *feelings*—only to control our *actions*. "Be ye angry, and sin not," says Paul (Eph. 4:26). It is *spiritual* to *show* feelings of anger, but *sinful* to be *controlled* by them.

The man who cannot control himself is precisely the one who seeks to control the lives of others. A man with no self-discipline will impose harsh rules upon his family. Having little spiritual power over himself, he reaches for power over others. Even friends, pastors, and business associates are not beyond his attempts to control.

When the Watergate tapes finally were made public, the public was shocked—not only at the illegal activities, but at the character of this country's leaders. Here were men who sought to rule the United States, but they could not rule their own tempers or their barracks-type language.

The spiritual man has no need to force super-spiritual control—people submit to him naturally. They seek his advice and follow his example because it seems good. They sense that his spirit is ruled by God's Spirit. Because *he* is controlled, he is allowed to control. Others submit to his authority because he is *under* authority.

Our Example

Read again Philippians 2:5-12, which was quoted in chapter 3. Paul says that Christ is our spiritual example. Christ the divine became a slave and died a criminal's death. He is exalted now *because of his slavery*, so that "every knee should bow . . . every tongue confess that Jesus Christ is Lord."

The spiritual man is just as comfortable washing dishes as he is when giving orders and advice. He is not miserable when someone else is right and he is proved wrong. The spiritual man can laugh, cry, admit fear, or be angry when the situation demands it.

I used to think that I was a very unemotional person. I was coldly logical, and I thought I could not change. Then a few events caused me to let down my guard and experience some emotions I did not know I had. Since then, I have been slowly releasing my grip on these emotions. Know what? As I experience these "forbidden" joys, hurts, and fears, I am losing fear of myself, and I like myself better.

Jesus expressed his feelings. He cried about Jerusalem and about his coming death on the cross. He attended a party, became angry with Peter, and was very tender with women. But he was always in control of his actions. We men think it unmanly to wash dishes; Jesus washed feet. We pastors think we must force our will on others; Jesus asks us to become our brother's slave.

C H A P T E R 8

Beyond Barbie and Ken

The Super-Spiritual Pastor and Family

*"I can't explain myself, I'm afraid, sir," said Alice, "because
I'm not myself you see."*
"I don't see," said the caterpillar.

—Lewis Carroll

My wife, Cheryl, and I were sitting in the living room,
having coffee with a new couple in the church. Tom and
Linda (not their real names) had been very shy and
withdrawn with us, but the barriers seemed to be
breaking down. We talked about our lives before meeting
Christ, and Cheryl and I also shared the problems and
joys of living the Christian life.

We spoke honestly and enthusiastically about our
family problems and our spiritual problems. As we told
them about the way the Lord was working in our lives,
the young couple gave us looks of fascination and
bewilderment.

Finally, Tom spoke. "When we first started coming to
your church, we thought you were the perfect couple.
We never imagined that you had problems; we thought
you were kind of like Barbie and Ken. I'm glad you're
not," he went on, "because I wondered for awhile if I was
really saved, what with all my problems."

How Are Ministers Supposed to Act?

When I assumed my first pastorate, I was given a great deal of advice. I have decided since that, for me, most of that advice will not work.

A good friend and fellow pastor took me aside and told me to avoid making friends in the congregation; that I should find friends among fellow pastors. A guest speaker at a training session for young ministers told us to "learn social distance." A book assigned by the district office told me what to wear (never let the congregation see you in sport clothes), how to act (with great dignity as befits your office), and what to say in almost any given situation.

The consensus was: "You were once just a person, but you are now a *minister* person—*act like one.*" The problem was that I did not *feel* any different; I did not feel like a minister.

Take, for instance, my telephone. I used to be able to answer with "Hello." Now I am supposed to say, "Good afternoon (or morning, or evening). Pastor Sterner speaking." I used to be able to stay home from church if I felt like it. Now I must be there (and sometimes I do *not* feel like it), because I am "the Pastor." I used to be able to spend time with whomever I pleased, just because I enjoyed their company. Now I worry that people may be jealous because I spend more time with "so-and-so" than with them.

"OK," you say, "but that comes with the job, just like late hours come with being a doctor and dirty hands with being a plumber." Maybe. And maybe not. I still do not like it. And when I do not like something, this is the first question I ask: Is this thing from God, or from the tradition of man? (If it *is* from God, I gotta *learn* to like it.)

Who's a Priest?

Under Old Testament regulations, the people of Israel were divided into two religious groups: priests and congregation. The function of the priesthood belonged to the tribe of Levi. If any member of the congregation wanted to reach God, he went to a priest. The priests sacrificed the animals, took care of the temple, burned the incense, sang in the choir, and generally were responsible for religious functions in the state of Israel. The congregation was responsible for the financial support of the priests.

The usual Old Testament rule was, If you need to contact God, get a priest. Saul became tired of waiting for Samuel and sacrificed burnt offerings himself; as a result, the kingdom was taken away from his family (I Sam. 13).

In the New Testament, the people of God no longer are called a congregation. They are called a church *(that which is called out),* a body, a temple, a bride, and a kingdom. In fact, in Revelation 1:6 (TEV), they are called a "kingdom of priests." Peter says that they are "a chosen generation a *royal priesthood"* (I Pet. 2:9, italics added).

Basically, the New Testament concept of a church is one in which there are many believer-priests, each ministering to God and to one another in his or her own way, as different parts of one Body in Christ. A priest may be assigned to teach or to be an evangelist, but that does not elevate that person to some kind of lofty position which demands more respect than do the other positions.

We hear a great deal about a "call to the ministry." I believe that it exists. I believe that I am called to be a pastor-teacher as described in the fourth chapter of Ephesians. (Did you know that that is the only time the word *pastor* in used in the New Testament?) I also believe that *you* are called to the ministry. Everyone who names the name of Christ has a "calling." And you will never be happy in God until you find out what that calling is and tell God that you will follow it.

Somewhere, though, between the book of Acts and the Middle Ages, the church began to make a distinction between *clergy* and *laity* (neither word is found in the

Bible). Pulpits were put on a platform, the pastor-teachers donned robes, began to abstain from marriage, and took the title of *priest*. Some years later, Martin Luther married, came down off the platform, and preached the priesthood of all believers, but it was too late.

You see, human nature being what it is, people would rather *hire* a priest than *be* one. It is so comfortable to be in the congregation. Priests must be religious. So we hire someone, pay a salary, and say, "You be religious for us. You be our priest." After all, *somebody* has to be spiritual.

Reverend Who?

Now, as I said before, I am no different with a "Reverend" on my name than I was without one. But there are different expectations put upon me now than when I was "congregation." I am expected to be on call twenty-four hours a day, cancel vacation plans to meet emergencies, always smile, wear a tie, and pray at all functions I happen to attend. In other words, I am supposed to be special—different from everybody else.

My wife is expected to function as a sort of unpaid associate pastor. She is supposed to attend (if not run) all women's meetings, visit the sick, keep a spotless house, teach Sunday school, shake hands with all visitors, and play the piano.

She and I do only a few of these things, much to the consternation of some of the members.

Most important (to me), I am not supposed to share my problems with my fellow priests. And according to a recent article in *Advance,* our ministers' magazine,

most preachers realize early the loneliness of the ministry. People confide in them, but they have no one, except perhaps a fellow minister, to turn to.

God knew the minister would face this problem and . . . invites us to cast every problem, burden, and confidence upon Him.

The next time you are tempted to confide in your most loyal member, remember the lesson so many have learned the hard way. When you feel you must talk to someone, talk to God. You have enough problems as it is; don't ask for more.

The most dangerous thing pastor-teachers can do is to begin to believe that they actually are as spiritual as the people think they are and sometimes demand that they be. No one is that spiritual. And this is the universal ministers' temptation—to become super-spiritual; to act as though we really are as good as the congregation thinks we are.

The Pastoral Hall of Fame

Consider, for instance, the "little dictator" pastor. No one ever dares to disagree with him. His sermons continually impress upon the members that the "man of God" is not to be disagreed with. They sing his favorite songs, celebrate his birthday, buy the version of the Bible he likes, and paint the church his favorite color. If he is crossed, he explodes, pouts, or threatens to leave. One speaker at a recent conference told us that he had requested seven families to leave his church (*his* church?).

Or how about the "entertainer" pastor, the one who keeps the service moving all the time? His church is filled with activities (all planned by him) and is open seven days a week. The people are so tired they could not contact God for themselves if they wanted to. Every hour is filled with choir practices, young people's groups, prayer meetings, family nights, visitations, or other activities. Gospel-music groups abound; evangelists are changed like handkerchiefs.

Then there is the "used-car salesman." This guy, like

the dictator, gets his own way, but he makes the members think it was their idea. Everything runs like clockwork. Smooth is the name of the game. . . . public relations . . . Madison Avenue. This pastor is always seen at the church-management seminars and the church-growth groups. He is always smiling, but ever in control.

Another funny duck is the "beggar." This one cries, pleads, begs the people to come to Christ, give to the building fund, and generally see things his way. No matter what the issue, he is whining. The members do not dare upset him or hurt his feelings by not doing what he wants.

How in the world did godly men sink so low? By super-spiritually trying to be the whole Body. By trying to copy a "successful" pastor. By not realizing that other people are ministers, too. These pastors need to discover their gifts and learn to function in the Body of Christ.

Who's the Church?

I constantly find myself in the trap of encouraging my people to worship. I exhort, I lead in song ("C'mon now, let's really hear it"). And if I am good enough, some will come to the altar and pray.

But on Wednesday night, at least, we do it differently. I open with a song and then toss the service out to the priesthood. If they do not do it, it does not get done. It is their responsibility to pray, sing, and testify. And when they are finished, I will teach. Sometimes our meetings are short, and sometimes they are long, but *we* are responsible for their length or their effectiveness. *We*, not *me!*

I refuse to *be* the church. I have come to lead, to teach,

63

and to guide the church into *their* ministry. The Bible says that pastors were given to the church "that Christians might be properly equipped for their service, that the whole body [of Christ] might be built up" (Eph. 4:12 Phillips). Why is the pastor supposed to do *all* the teaching, *all* the visiting, and *all* the administrative work of the church? Could not the Lord raise up other men and women to help? Help!!

I also refuse to be like the previous pastor, or like any other pastor. I find that when I let a church squeeze me into a mold, I become moldy. For years the members have told me, "You're different," and I say, "Thank you!" I intend to remain different, myself, me.

I further refuse to be alone in the kingdom of priests. I need to talk to people about my needs, my hang-ups, my dreams. I need friends. And if I cannot find those friends in the church, then the church is not what it claims to be—a fellowship of love.

Do I have problems because I refuse to do these things? *Yes!* There are people who do not understand; people who are afraid to be my friends and who are jealous of those who are not afraid; pressures from without and within to conform, to get with the program. But I happen to feel that I can cope better with those problems than with the knowledge that I am a super-spiritual phony.

"If I Should Die Before I Wake"

Super-Spiritual Christians and Death

Death is always and under all circumstances a tragedy, for if it is not, then it means that life itself has become one.
—Theodore Roosevelt

How is a Christian supposed to act when someone dies? As a pastor, I am asked this question often. Not in so many words—not right out—but subtly, with the eyes and the tone of voice. When you really think about it, this is an amazing question. The words *dead* and *death* are used almost seven hundred times in the Bible. Jesus, Paul, James, and John all talk about death, but Christians do not seem to know how to handle it.

"Of all the wonders that I yet have heard," says Shakespeare's *Julius Caesar* (Act II, sc. 2), "It seems to me most strange that men should fear;/Seeing that death, a necessary end,/Will come when it will come." But fear it we do, all of us. "Men fear death as children fear to go in the dark," commented Francis Bacon. Fear of death is fear of the unknown, the mysterious, the dark.

Of course, Christians have an inside advantage over other people. We know of the only Man who ever came back from the grave. But even Jesus did not tell us very much about how it felt to die, or what day-to-day life in heaven is like.

We are left, then, with a very unhappy reality: All of us are afraid to die, and we will do almost anything possible to prolong life. And that is the way God planned it. If one were *not* afraid to die, one might be tempted to commit suicide every time things went drastically wrong.

Christians Are Not Afraid of Death . . . ?

But we have been trained by well-meaning Sunday school teachers and Christian friends that fear of death is unspiritual. "Death, where is thy sting? O grave, where is thy victory?" (I Cor. 15:56) is quoted frequently, as is "God hath not given us the spirit of fear; but of power, and of love, and of a sound mind" (II Tim. 1:7).

We hear this and we say to ourselves, "I must be very unspiritual if I am so afraid of death. I will keep a stiff upper lip about it." I visit people in the hospital who know they are dying and who want so very much to cry. They want to say, Why me? to God, but instead they smile and talk about the streets of gold and the mansions over the hilltop. Their friends whisper to each other, "Isn't she taking it well?" And when visiting hours are over, the dying weep quietly, bitterly, and alone.

When a loved one dies, I want to comfort the family. But since I am super-spiritual about death, I know that we must say only good things about it. So I quote Romans 8:28 (the very *worst* verse to quote to a person in emotional pain), and I say something stupid like, "I know how you feel now, but you'll get over it."

Go Ahead and Cry

Jesus cried at funerals (John 11:35). Paul tells us to "weep with them that weep" (Rom. 12:15). Let's face it, when a loved one dies, people hurt. They hurt because they miss the person; because they feel guilty about not baving treated the person better or about not visiting when the loved one was alive. But they also hurt inside for another reason. Something they had pushed back into a small dark corner of their soul—something they tried to forget about and pretended was not there— suddenly has thrust itself obnoxiously into the very center of their being. "You, too, will die someday."

What, then, are we to do with death? Cry! Admit that we are scared, hurt, bitter. Do away with the super-spiritual facade that smiles at everyone and cries itself to sleep at night. For heaven's sake, and for the sake of our own mental health, we must admit that we are afraid of death. Not as afraid as the heathen, perhaps, but afraid, nonetheless. By this means, and by this means alone, can we ever hope to become less afraid and more spiritual.

Jeanette W. Lockerbie tells the story of a minister whose wife had died unexpectedly. The church, at his insistence, had a gay "memorial service"; everybody dressed in bright clothing and praised God that their loved one was in heaven. No sorrow was allowed and no tears were present.

Some weeks later, the reaction began to set in. This hitherto vital, decisive man appeared to withdraw into a fog. People close to him found this difficult to understand. He had taken his wife's death so well he hadn't broken down once! Not knowing quite how to handle his silences and frequent remoteness, people shied away from Rev. Williams, leaving him alone with his gnawing grief. He was expected to share the burdens of his congregations, yet he himself found scarcely anyone with whom he could unburden his crying heart. (*How to Be a Saint While Lying Flat on Your Back,* ed. William Peterson)

*If We
Don't Look at It . . .*

We are afraid of death, and so we hide it. We hide it in nursing homes, in hospitals, and in funeral chapels.

Most of us never have watched a person die. (Until recent years, most of us never had been allowed to watch one being born, either.) And because we hide death, it frightens us even more.

Recently, my five-year-old daughter asked to accompany my wife and me to a funeral home. Automatically, I said, "Honey, you don't want to go there." Then I realized that she *did* want to go there, and I took her. While my wife and I comforted the family as best we could, Joy went right up to the coffin and stared at the dead body of the woman she had known. As a matter of fact, she stared so long that I became embarrassed. When we left, she took my hand and said, "Well, *that* wasn't so bad, was it?"

And the truth is, death is *not* so bad, if you look it right in the face. But we never do. Consider all the different ways we can say "Mary died." We say that she passed away or went to her reward, her eternal rest, her home over yonder. She did not really die, we say; she began the great adventure, crossed over Jordan, climbed the last mountain, gave up the ghost.

Well, for my five-year-old, Mary had died. When I tried to tell Joy that Mary was not really there, she said, "Oh yes, she was; I *saw* her." Let's face it—for us, the living, Mary really is dead and gone. And we hurt like everything.

A friend of mine, a cancer specialist, told me, "I've never met anyone who couldn't take the news that he was dying of cancer. What they *can't* take is *not knowing.*" I hereby go on record in this controversy as saying, "Tell them everything!" Nowhere in the Bible does it instruct us to speak a lie in love. We must tell them they are dying. And then cry with them. Unless we want to be super-spiritual-and-brave-and-phony.

CHAPTER 10

Everybody But Me and Thee

Super-Spiritual Christians Are Never Wrong

I may not always be right, but I am never wrong.
—Anonymous

In the past ten years, I have counseled and pastored hundreds of people. And few of them ever had a problem! I have talked to depressed mothers, alcoholics, runaway kids, and dope pushers. All of them shared one thing. They all blamed someone else for the mess they were in. Someone *else* always had the problem.

If you were to listen to recordings of our conversations, you would hear the following phrases: If only my parents would get off my back; if only my wife would stop nagging me; if only my husband would get a job. If only—her mother . . . my boss . . . the kids . . . the pastor . . . the congregation . . . and so on, ad infinitum and ad nauseam.

But here is the classic: Why is God doing this to me? When we run out of people to blame, we blame God. Why does he allow this unfair thing to happen to me? "If he loved me as much as you *say* he does," said one client recently, "he would *do* something about the mess I'm in!" Why do we continually blame God, parents, and others for our problems? Because of our tremendous need to be right.

There seems to be a universal desire on the part of humankind to be always right. We want very badly, almost desperately, to be right about religion, politics, sports, moral questions . . . the list is endless. "I was wrong once," said a comedian. "Back in 1952 I thought I was mistaken, and it turned out I wasn't."

This pathological need to be right at all costs seems to be present in all classes of people. Men and women, rich or poor, religious or nonreligious—all want to be on the right side. You might think that education would dispel this notion, but strangely enough, it seems to strengthen it. Says James Barnes, "You can always tell a Harvard man, but you cannot tell him much."

But surely, religion should help to eliminate our need to be always right. The Bible gives us so many examples of great men who sometimes were wrong. The children of Israel seldom obeyed God. Paul continually corrected theological disputes and personal quarrels. But Christians seem to have a marvelous ability to ignore these lessons. "When most men say 'I am thinking about it,' they are merely rearranging their prejudices," commented Donald Gray Barnhouse.

To start an argument, simply gather together a few good members of different Bible-believing churches. Then ask a few questions: When will the rapture occur? Do you speak in tongues? What is the correct way to baptize?

Now, I have my doctrinal beliefs and I think they are right. But there are other sincere Christians who disagree with me. I am forced to admit that when I arrive in heaven I may find that a good number of my cherished beliefs were wrong! So I refuse to argue religion. I am willing to discuss my beliefs with anyone who really cares, but super-spiritual people do not listen. They only wait for others to shut up so that they can correct their errors.

Super-spiritual people just want to argue, and the Bible says we should avoid that. "Warn them before God against quarreling about words," admonished Paul. "It is of no value, and only ruins those who listen" (II Tim. 2:14

NIV). He further advised Timothy to "steer clear of foolish discussions which lead . . . to anger" (2:16 TLB).

Love?
Or Need?

This obsessive desire to be right leads Christians to attack other Christians under the banner of doctrinal purity. It also causes Christians to attack non-Christians under the banner of evangelism. Harry Golden wrote:

> I am puzzled by the letters and pamphlets I receive from Christian and Christian-Hebrew mission groups urging me to join, and become a convert. I am also puzzled by the vast sums of money appropriated by many church organizations for the purpose of carrying on this mission work. The downtown Luncheon Club I cannot join.
> If they don't want me for one hour at the Luncheon Club, why should they seek my companionship in heaven through all eternity? *(Only in America)*

Is it Christian love for this Jewish man that leads us to send him all those letters and pamphlets? Or is it our need to put him down and assert our righteousness? I really believe that those without a relationship to God through Christ will go to hell. But I *also* believe that attacking a person's beliefs is the quickest way to strengthen those beliefs. No one wants to be proved wrong.

In *How to Win Friends and Influence People*, Dale Carnegie tells the story of the capture of the notorious killer, Two-Gun Crowley, who would kill at the drop of a hat. While one hundred fifty police officers fired bullets and tear gas into his apartment, Crowley composed a letter. "Under my coat is a weary heart," said the letter, "but a kind one—one that would do nobody any harm." He was finally sentenced to the electric chair for the murder of a policeman who had asked to see his driver's license.

Carnegie goes on to tell about Dutch Schultz, another gangster, who called himself a public benefactor, and about Al Capone, who once said, "I have spent the best years of my life giving people the lighter pleasures, helping them have a good time, and all I get is abuse." Concludes Carnegie, "If you want to gather honey, don't kick over the beehive."

Look at Job. Four of his good buddies gather around, telling him he has missed God, has fallen into unforgivable sin, or at least is being punished by the Almighty. But not once does Job admit to any wrongdoing until he is confronted by God himself. I think this contains a lesson for evangelism (and other arguments). <u>Never take a person any farther than he is prepared to go.</u>

There is no "canned plan" of evangelism that will make someone come to Christ if he or she does not want to. People need to be confronted by God himself. He will cut through all their blaming and excuses, straight into the core of their being. "Once have I spoken; but I will not answer," said Job after hearing from God. "Yea, twice; but I will proceed no further. . . . I have heard of thee by the hearing of the ear: but now mine eye seeth thee. Wherefore I abhor myself, and repent in dust and ashes" (Job 40:5, 42:5-6).

Jesus said that no man can come to him unless the Father draws him (John 6:44). I believe in aggressive evangelism. I do *not* believe in being pushy when a person is not interested. It is the Holy Spirit's job, not mine, to convince men of their sin (John 16:8).

Courage to Admit Mistakes

W<small>HEN I AM RIGHT</small>, declares a poster, <small>NO ONE REMEMBERS. WHEN I AM WRONG, NO ONE FORGETS.</small> Whenever you make a mistake, there is always a temptation to hide it. If you admit your fault, you will be in for criticism, perhaps ridicule. If you hide it, perhaps no one will ever find out what you did. But chances are, if you try to hide your error, you will cause yourself a lot of extra trouble.

Mistakes always cost something. "Be sure your sin will find you out" (Num. 32:23). Even if no one else knows, *you* do. All the denials and rationalizations in the world will not change that. Furthermore, you always will be haunted by the fear that someone *might* find out. The answer? Simple—admit that you blew it!

Besides, "A man should never be ashamed to own he has been in the wrong," says Harry Brown, since owning it only shows that "he is wiser today than he was yesterday." It takes courage to admit you were wrong— but isn't that what courage is for?

Every so often, someone will tell me that he has committed the unpardonable sin. He does not know what the unpardonable sin *is,* exactly, but he is sure that he did it. I never have found a person yet who was guilty of such sin, but I *do* know of one type of sin that *is* unpardonable—*unconfessed* sin. "If we confess our sins, he is faithful and just to forgive us our sins, and to cleanse us from all unrighteousness" (I John 1:9).

I am not talking about the issue of eternal life. I am talking about the here-and-now abundant life that Jesus promised. If we refuse to admit wrong, we separate ourselves from any chance of peace with ourselves or with God.

When our mistakes occur (and they *will* occur), we can be super-spiritual and pretend they never happened. Or we can be truly spiritual—admit our mistakes, try to find out *why* they happened, and see what can be done to keep them from happening again. Perhaps we were using wrong methods or false logic. A small change might be made in our thinking or habits that would completely eliminate these kinds of errors.

God Is Not Mean

God really is not interested in punishing us. He is interested only in helping us prevent the same thing from happening again. If we know why a mistake happened, and perhaps how it could have been prevented, we can save time, effort, and worry by immediately saying, "I blew it."

The more quickly a mistake is caught and corrected, the less costly it will be. Christians with the honesty and courage to spot their errors and report them to God and to others are doing themselves a big favor. People will appreciate this attitude so much that they will tend to forget the mistake.

"He that covereth his sins shall not prosper: but whoso confesseth and forsaketh them shall have mercy" (Prov. 28:13). My wife insists that Adam was the first tattletale. "Did you eat from the tree I told you to leave alone?" asks God. "The woman *you gave me, she* gave it to me." Adam blames Eve and slyly implicates God himself. "What have you done?" God asks Eve. "The snake tricked me," says Eve. "The devil made me do it" (Sterner Version). I would love to know who the snake blamed.

Who's God?

This intense striving to be right, this pathological denial of our sin, this angry blaming of others reveals yet a deeper sin. We want to be like God . . . no, we want to *be* God. We would supplant the Almighty, we would be "captain of our fate, master of our souls."

"How art thou fallen from heaven, O Lucifer, son of the morning! . . . For thou hast said in thine heart, I will ascend into heaven, I will exalt my throne above the stars of God. . . . I will ascend above the heights of the clouds; *I will be like the most High*" (Isa. 14:12-14, italics added). Helmut Thielicke writes:

The hour of temptation is the hour in which we believe in ourselves, in which we cease to doubt ourselves, and therefore doubt God. . . . Now we understand why man is tested and tempted from the beginning: because he believes in himself.

And we understand at last the meaning of the words "man is in temptation." He is constantly on the point of becoming unfaithful to God; he constantly desires to be free of God.

This wish to be free of God is the deepest yearning of man. It is greater than his yearning for God. *(Between God and Satan)*

"God says we mustn't eat it [the fruit] or even touch it, or we will die," said Eve. "That's a lie!" the serpent hissed. "You'll not die. God knows very well that the instant you eat it *you will become like him*" (Gen. 3:3-5 TLB, italics added). Here is super-spirituality at its core—looking for the quick and easy way to be like God. The spiritual man knows there *is* no easy way. We are to be slowly, sometimes painfully "conformed to the image" of Christ (Rom. 8:29).

We want the right things, but in the wrong order. We want to be like God; that is, we want to be powerful, knowledgeable, and respected. We want the *glory* of God. God, too, wants us to be like him, and he promises that we will be (I John 3:2). But God wants us to be like him in loving, suffering, giving, and patience, first; the glory will come later.

We are like the man who prayed, "Lord, I want patience, and I want it *now!*" And if we do not get it now, we will *pretend* to have it now. When we believe ourselves to be always right, we believe ourselves to be God. People do it, churches do it, and Satan did it. But that's the company super-spirituality keeps.

Fifty thousand Frenchmen *can* be wrong. And so can you. If you grasp the freedom that allowing yourself to be wrong gives you, you may just leap for joy! No more worrying about defending hopeless positions or fearing the shame of being laughed at when finally found out. No more hanging on when you would really like to let go and change. Unless, of course, you are super-spiritual— and never wrong.

C H A P T E R 1 1

I'm Just Awful

Super-Spiritual Humility

> *One man pretends to be rich,*
> *yet has nothing;*
> *another pretends to be poor,*
> *yet has great wealth.* —*Proverbs 13:7 (NAB)*

Tom huddled up in the corner of my office and tried to make himself small. He looked at me only when he thought I was not looking at him, and his face was hidden behind his hand. We were talking about his favorite subject—how terrible he was.

"I'm a mess, pastor," he said. "A real zero. I mean, I never do anything right, and I'm always in trouble. I guess there's no hope. I don't know why God made me, anyhow!"

"You certainly are hard on yourself," I answered (I didn't know what else to say). "How come you hate yourself so much?"

"Well, let me put it this way," he joked bitterly. "If I knew someone like me, I'd never be seen with him.

In many ways, Tom is typical of many Christians who come to my office for help. He is depressed. He is bored. He often lies around the house for hours at a time, doing nothing. He has considered suicide. He has watched so much television he finds it difficult to distinguish between fantasy and reality.

He Learned
Self-Hate

Tom is full of anger, depression, anxiety, and rebellion. He is also a Christian; therefore, he vacillates furiously between periods of booze, sex, and drugs and times of self-condemnation and breast-beating. He will tell off teachers and break all the rules at home; then suddenly he will be meekly subservient to everyone. He is almost never happy.

What Tom needs, of course, is to learn to like himself. He must appreciate being Tom and feel good about himself if he is ever to break the cycle of rebellion and self-hate. His church could help greatly, for in spite of what he says, he does listen to the church. His church, however, does not help him—it only intensifies the problem.

Pride and conceit were the original sin of man, according to our Church Fathers. Satan was guilty of pride when he wanted to "be like the most High." "From pride, vainglory and hypocrisy . . . Good Lord deliver us," pleads the Book of Common Prayer. "Pride goeth before destruction, and a haughty spirit before a fall," cautions the proverb. We have been so warned against pride that we instantly recoil in defense when someone dares to accuse us of it.

To be humble is a great virtue. It is "the way to honour" (Prov. 15:33 NEB). It is "a virtue all preach but none practice," according to John Seldon. Paul urges us to "put on therefore, as the elect of God . . . humbleness of mind [and] meekness" (Col. 3:12). William Cowper sums it up this way: "Knowledge is proud that he has learned so much; wisdom is humble that he knows no more."

You get the message? Proud is bad news; humble is

where it's at. Jesus described himself as "meek and lowly in heart" (Matt. 11:29). Sooo . . . since I am supposed to "be conformed to the image" of Christ (Rom. 8:29), I gotta be humble. And if I do not feel humble, I will fake it.

Fake Humility

Sunday was the most predictable day of the week when I was a small boy. We ate eggs instead of cereal for breakfast, read the funnies, and went to Sunday school. After church, we would hurry across town to have Sunday dinner at Grandma's. Grandma always had roast beef for dinner and it was always great! However, she invariably brought the roast to the table with the same words: "Oh dear, I'm afraid the roast is tough." Grandpa would then respond liturgically, "It's tougher when there ain't any."

It did not matter that, for years, the roast always had been great. It did not matter that we were too hungry to care, anyway. It did not matter that my grandmother had a B.A. in home economics from Michigan State and had taught cooking at Central High for years. Each week it was, "Oh dear, I'm afraid the roast is tough," with the inevitable reply from Grandpa.

What did Grandma gain from this weekly Sunday charade? A lot! Every member of the family would make a special effort to assure her that the meal in general, and the roast in particular, was unequaled, inimitable, unparalleled. And Grandma would fret, smile shyly, and hesitantly ask, "Are you sure?" She was a master at the art of false humility.

"One may be humble out of pride," writes Montaigne, "and the best virtue I have has in it some tincture of vice." Can it be possible that there is a selfish motive behind my grandma's humbleness, Tom's, and even mine? What possible reasons could we have?

Reason 1—Attention

If I continually point out to you how awful I am, perhaps you will play the game by telling me how good I am. Grandma, of course, is a good example, and so is Tom. Then there is the athlete who "shoulda done better," the lady who never can receive a compliment without telling you how old the dress is or how little it costs. Or how about the embarrassment I feel when someone tells me they liked my sermon?

Some people play this attention game to the limit. Usually, they are persons who were ignored by busy parents early in life. They learned that the only sure way to get attention was to persuade someone to feel sorry for them. "I'm afraid to lose my problems," moaned a woman in my office. "Who would I be without them? Who would pay attention to me if I were not depressed?"

But why manipulate attention? Why not come right out and demand it? Because we have been told that asking for attention is wrong; that really spiritual people do not do that. But the fact is that *everyone* wants and needs attention and tries to get it in a variety of ways. It would be better for Grandma to gain attention honestly, but since she wants so very much to be humble, this is out of the question. So she, like so many of us, obtains it dishonestly, with false humility.

Reason 2—An Excuse for Inactivity

Once upon a time, there was a boy who was lazy. Knowing that laziness displeased his parents, and yet loathing work, he was in a dilemma. "How," he pondered, "can I manage to get out of my responsibilities without incurring the wrath of Mommy and Daddy?" He tried one thing after another: He made excuses, he cried, he threw temper tantrums, but nothing worked.

Then one day (quite by accident) the boy discovered a foolproof technique for avoiding his duties. He came upon a job that was unfamiliar to him, and he was, of course, momentarily confused. "Oh my goodness, Mommy," he blurted out. "I could *never* do *that*." And there it was—the manipulative key to his future. His mother immediately came charging to the rescue. "Of course you can't, darling," she gushed. "How could I ever have asked you to? Mommy will do it—don't you fret."

From that day until this—whether in school, at work, with his friends or family, or in my office—the boy has used this highly successful form of manipulation. Whenever he encounters anything new, distasteful, threatening, or simply difficult, he folds up like a road map. "I just can't do that!" he whines constantly. "I'm just not strong enough, I don't have it in me, I just can't. Oh, I'm so awful!"

Now, I realize that for our own good, we had better recognize our limitations. "I cannot fly like a bird," says psychologist Clyde Narramore, "and to try would be to court constant failure and depression." But most people who say "I just can't" are *really* saying "I just *won't*." I won't try because I never did it before, and I might *fail* (oh, horrors!). Besides, if I tried and *did* succeed, people might expect me to try other nasty things as well. They might (perish the thought) expect me to grow up!

Reason 3—I Look So Spiritual (super-spiritual, in fact)

After all, I am supposed to be conforming to the image of Christ. And Jesus was so humble . . . or was he? Not very, if you use the super-spiritual definition. When Jesus was about twelve, he thought himself adequate to debate theology with the Jewish masters. Shortly after his thirtieth birthday, he convinced a group of men (some of them successful businessmen) to drop what they were doing and follow him. He demanded that they not look back to their homes, families, or occupations, but give total allegiance to him. He did this on no authority other than his own name.

Jesus was always announcing his identity to anyone

who would listen: I am the way, the truth, and the life.
. . . I am the light of the world. . . . I am the bread of life.
. . . I am the true vine, the good shepherd, the door, the
resurrection, and the life. . . . I and my Father are one.
This is humble?

Toward a Definition of Humility

These "I ams" would sound ludicrous, insane, in my
mouth or yours. Coming from the mouth of Jesus, they
sound plausible, even logical—why? Because he *was* the
light of the world, the bread of life, and the good
shepherd. He was exactly what he said he was. Are you?
If I were to ask you about yourself, would you tell me
honestly? Or would you tell me only the good things?
That is pride. On the other hand, if you tell me only the
bad things, that is false humility—super-spirituality.
True humility exists when we agree with God about who
we are.

"OK," you say, "but I *see* only bad things. So *now* what
do I do?" For many of us, this is all too painfully true. The
task, then, is to stop looking at yourself through the eyes
of others and start looking through the eyes of God. It is
not important what your friends think, or what your
mother told you, or what I think. It is not even important
what *you* think about yourself. But it is vitally important
that you discover what God thinks about you.

✓ What Does God Think About You?

First of all, God created you in his image. You got that?
He created probably ten million varieties of insects; one
or two billion stars in our galaxy (scientists estimate that
there may be several billion galaxies); but *only one you!*
And the person that is you is somehow like God! That

81

person can think, feel, plan, decide, create. Nothing else in the universe does that.

"Thou hast made him a little lower than the angels, and hast crowned him with glory and honour" (Ps. 8:5). Did all you "grandmas" hear that? When I humbly agree with my Creator, I meekly assert that my person is glorious, honorable, and just a hair below angelhood. Did you know, for instance, that a computer capable of doing all the things the human brain does would need to be the size of a skyscraper?

Second, God has given each of us a part to play in the governing of his universe. Genesis 1:26 and Psalm 8:6 declare that God gave man dominion over all the earth. The fact that we have ruled poorly does not diminish this fact; the responsibility of ruling the earth is still ours. Not only that, but Paul tells us in First Corinthians 6:3 that someday we shall be in charge of angels! Ponder *that* for an hour or so and see if your head does not swell a bit.

Third, each of us is unique. The *Encyclopaedia Britannica* tells us that no two snowflakes ever are alike. Now, it takes thousands of snowflakes just to make one snowball, and tons of snow have fallen each year for thousands of years. I do not understand how anyone can prove that no two snowflakes ever have been alike, but I know this—*no two people ever are alike!*

Wouldn't it be great if we all really believed that? No one would ever say, "Why can't you be like your brother?" or "You're just like your father." The reason that I am not just like my brother, father, or pastor is because I am not *supposed* to be. I am unique. I am *me!* Why? So that I can fit together with all of you into the Body of Christ.

How to Have a Crummy Christmas

Just imagine a five-year-old boy who opens a Christmas present and finds a big can of tinker toys. He is so happy, so excited, so thrilled!—until he opens the can and finds that he has 462 three-inch red sticks. There are no little orange balls with holes in them, no wheels, no short yellows or long purples—just 462 medium reds! "Whadda ya expect me to do with these?" he wails. "I can't *build* anything!"

Yet we all want to be like someone else. If only I could preach like he does, sing like she does—look like, be as smart as, as rich as, as popular or as together as. The list is endless. But how can God build anything out of a church if it were composed of 462 duplicates? If I want to fit together with you in order to build something, I had better find out what God wants me to be like; I had better find out how you and I can join together.

I Don't Wanna

The problem is that I do not really *want* to fit into God's plan; I want *him* to fit into *mine*. I do not want to be that part that I was designed to be, because it is not *important* enough (according to me). I do not want to be the big toe in the Body of Christ; I want to be the *mouth*. *I want to be* SOMEBODY!

So here I am trying to become somebody (else) through imitation. And God is saying, "John, you don't have to *become* somebody; you *are* somebody. You cannot be any more important than you are. I died for you, and that makes you important." So I vacillate between peace of mind in knowing my value to God, and worry in suspecting my low value to other people.

Christians are the only people in the world who have any lasting purpose in life. The fame, money, or power that I work so hard to gain lasts for a few years; then time snatches it away. Spiritual reality lasts forever. If I begin to find my role in the Body of Christ, I am laying up permanent treasures in heaven (Matt. 6:19).

Because Christ lives in me, God is willing to give me

glory. Webster defines *glory* as having to do with *fame, importance, value,* and *honor.* The glory of the Lord in the Old Testament was so overpowering that strong men often fell to their knees in fear. People could not bear even to look at Moses when his face shone with God's glory.

"All of us who are Christians have no veils on our faces, but reflect like mirrors the glory of the Lord" (II Cor. 3:18 Phillips). I am honorable. I am valuable, famous, and important. I am glorious because God lives in me. Take away that treasure and I am left with Paul's "earthen vessel," whose righteousness is like filthy rags. But *God* has *not* been taken away; he is here. And I am *glorious!*

If I state my glory openly, however, I will run the risk of censure by those unwilling to state theirs. I am usually too afraid of their rejection to state it openly, which would be real humility, so I settle for false humility. My problem? I care more about what others think of me than about what God thinks of me. Do not allow anyone to "cheat you . . . by wanting you to join him in false humility," says Paul (Col. 2:18 Phillips). Amen!

C H A P T E R   1 2

I'll Start Next Monday

The Curse of Procrastination

The rule is, jam tomorrow, and jam yesterday—but never jam today. 　　　　　　　　　　　　*—Lewis Carroll*

You readers probably do not notice anything different about this chapter. But there is—there is a big difference. This chapter is three years newer than the last one.

I really do not know what happened; I was working right along, banging out chapter after chapter when . . . I just quit. It did not matter that my friends liked what I had written so far and urged me to continue. It did not matter that I had no real excuse for not writing. It did not matter that a publisher had expressed interest in the first few chapters. I just quit. Did you ever do that?

This is very hard for me; I want to share with you the distress, the pain, and the super-spirituality of having that manuscript on the shelf and not working on it. I want to let you know how much I wanted to start again, but didn't. I want to confide in you, I think, more than I know. I really am not sure why I stopped. For that matter, I do not know why I started again, either. But since I cannot locate the precise reason, let me give you the excuses.

How Dare You?

First of all, all the publishers hurt my feelings. They actually wanted me to make some changes! I had worked hard, and now some faceless editor (probably some little old lady in tennis shoes) wanted to tamper with my work of art. Who did they think they were, anyway?

Proverbs 24:26 says, "An honest answer is a sign of true friendship" (TEV). Instead of accepting that honest answer, I pouted. "What do they know?" I sulked. "Seest thou a man wise in his own conceit? There is more hope of a fool than of him" (Prov. 26:12).

Second, I was very busy. I "didn't have time" to write. I made sure I was busy doing the right things, too! I preached, I visited, I counseled, and I went on lecture tours. I read books and journals. I went to seminars, and even spent some time with my family. Whenever God spoke softly to me, urging me to write, I would say, "I'm too busy working for you, God. I'm so busy doing your work that I can't write anything now. I'll start it soon, though—maybe next Monday when I have a day off."

I never could shake the feeling of hypocrisy, though, when I was busying myself in some project in order to escape. Psalm 127:1-2 (TEV) says:

> If the Lord does not build the house,
>   the work of the builders is useless;
> if the Lord does not protect the city,
>   it does no good for the sentries to stand guard.
> It is useless to work so hard for a living,
>   getting up early and going to bed late.

That's how I feel when I am doing a "work for the Lord" that isn't really the Lord's work—useless.

To Do or Not to Do

Have you ever noticed that you always have enough time to do the things you really want to do? That you usually arrive on time at the places you really want to go? And that you rarely forget those things that are really important to you? So why are some things so easy to forget, so hard to finish?

When some project becomes distasteful to you, although there is great pressure on you to complete it, you can respond to the project in one of three different ways. First, you can openly chuck the project and deal with the guilt, blame, or whatever consequences result. Second, you can grit your teeth and finish the project. Or you may respond in a third way, as I did, with what psychologists call passive-aggressive behavior.

Passive-aggressive behavior is anything that I can do to effectively kill a project without being blamed for the failure. It is largely subconscious in nature—that is, I do it without being aware that I am doing it. Passive-aggressive behavior may express itself in forgetfulness, consistent lateness, "stupid" mistakes, clumsiness, or, in my case, procrastination. "Pretty soon," I promised myself for three years, "I'll sit down and get cracking again."

A War Within

According to Fritz Perls' *Gestalt Therapy Verbatim*, the situation is as if two people were inside me, sniping at each other. One is a big-boss type whom Dr. Perls calls Top-dog. Top-dog is a bully who shouts and demeans others to get his way. His opponent is Under-dog, a sneaky little guy who uses passive-aggressive behavior as Bobby Fisher uses chess men. Both dogs are me, and both want to win.

"Shape up and get this book finished," yells Top-dog. "You should have written two or three books by now. What's the matter with you, anyhow, you jerk?"

"I will, I will," promises Under-dog, "but I'm busy

right now and I really don't have any fresh ideas. And besides, I don't feel so good. Next Monday, though, I'll get right on it." Dr. Perls says that Under-dog almost always wins and that in the long run, Monday comes and goes.

So why is my Under-dog subverting this book? Heaven knows I am not lazy. If anything, I work too hard. Although writing is not one of my favorite activities, I do enjoy the finished product. So what is wrong with me? Super-spiritualism. I want to *be* an author, not *become* one. As long as my book is on the shelf, as long as I am in the *process* of writing, I am an author. When it is completed, when people read it and judge it, I may be a hack.

What if no one will print it? What if they *do* print it, and the critics don't like it? (Or worse, ignore it.) What if nobody buys it? But as long as it sits on the shelf in process, I am an author, if only in my dreams. I can tell people about the book I am working on that may be a big success someday—the one I plan to get back to soon. When I have more time. Maybe next Monday.

·

CHAPTER 13

Who Is Leading Whom?

Super-Spiritual Guidance

Let God be God.   —*Dick Eastman*

Some time ago, a young lady dropped into my office with a big problem. After a short session of counseling, she left, exclaiming, "I just know that God has sent me to you! You seem to understand me *so* much better than any of the others." The "others" turned out to be her own pastor, her husband, and several psychiatrists and counselors. She came twice. When I called her to see why she had missed the third session, she explained that "God has led me to another counselor," and she thanked me very much for my trouble.

Now, that experience made me angry. But not angry enough to print it in a book just to get even with her. What *really* burned me up is that this illustrates a problem that is so common among Christians: super-spiritual "leading."

Here is how it works. Suppose you want to do something, but you have no logical reason for doing it. You really want to do it; your feelings are almost *screaming* for you to do it. Yet at the same time, you can hear the voices of friends, relatives, and pastors asking, "Why did you do that?" So you are caught in a double bind—wanting to do something and wanting to be able to come up with a reasonable explanation after you have done it.

The
Way Out

"I just wanted to" sounds too selfish. If you say, "I don't know why I did it," you look like a dummy, while the old standard "I couldn't help myself" will get you only pity. Fortunately, there is a phrase that not only will get you off the hook, but will make you seem strong, confidently spiritual, a person to be admired: "God led me to do it."

These words, pronounced with clarity and strong assurance, are guaranteed to stop your opponents in their tracks. The gullible will believe you implicitly. Non-Christians will not believe, but will not know what to say. Other Christians will be in various states of belief and disbelief—but who can criticize God?

Now, you may become tired of that one phrase. So here are some other ways to say it: The Spirit spoke to my heart. . . . God told me. . . . The Lord is showing me. . . . Jesus wants me to. Any of these sentences that fit the occasion and your nature may be used. All are sure criticism-stoppers.

I hesitated before including this chapter. I was under the impression that the only people who played this super-spiritual game were pentecostals and charismatics like myself. We have visions, dreams, prophecies, and the like, on a regular basis. But some of my friends of other evangelical persuasions assure me that this problem runs amok through their churches, too. "When in doubt, blame God," seems to be the byword of the day.

God
Leads His Way

Now for the hard part: Do I really believe that God ever speaks to or leads people? After all, the Bible is full of such speakings and leadings. Moses spoke to the Almighty "face to face." Gideon saw an angel, and Elijah heard a "still small voice." Paul and Barnabas were "set apart by the Holy Spirit." Jesus promised that his sheep would hear his voice and be led by him. Am I a heretic?

Don't Stone Me, Please

I am not a heretic and I do believe that God leads me supernaturally. I just do *not* believe that all "leadings" are from God. I question the leadings, for instance, of super-spiritual butterflies. Those are the people who flit from prayer meeting, to church, to revival—from blessing to blessing—never staying long enough to come under the authority of the church or to do any work for it.

I just do not believe those people who become angry and leave a church, and then say, "The Lord is leading me onward." It seems odd to me that all those leadings seem to be down the path the person wanted to take in the first place! Not so with our Bible heroes!

Moses did not want to return to Egypt. Gideon was scared to death of the Philistines. Elijah was hiding in fear for his life when he was ordered to go back. Paul wanted to go to Asia, but instead was ordered to minister in Europe. It seems to me that God pretty much leaves people alone when they are going to do what he wants anyway. He seems to intervene most often when he wants them to change their plans and do what they do not want to do.

I have trouble with some super-spiritual leadings on two counts. First, as I have already pointed out, they seem to be our way of manipulating God. That is, we want a thing; therefore God wants us to have it. My second problem is that so many of these leadings are

91

hard to understand. In fact, some of them are just plain dumb.

God's Ways
Are Not Our Ways—
But They're No Dumber Than Ours

Consider the afore-mentioned young lady. She never really receives counseling at all. She merely runs from ear to ear, telling her story, which means that she never receives help (which is precisely what she wants). Or think about the couple in my office who were married, but not to each other. "God has led us to be together," they cooed.

Yes, I know the Scripture tells us, "My thoughts are not your thoughts, neither are your ways my ways, saith the Lord." But neither are his ways absurd. Leaving for the moment the "repent and be pardoned" context of Isaiah 53:8, let me admit that many of the ways of God seem *at the moment* to be a bit strange. In retrospect, however, God's ways always make sense.

Gideon won with three hundred men and some torches. Joshua marched and walls fell down. Elijah prayed and fire consumed his water-soaked wood. Paul went to Jerusalem, was thrown into jail, and wrote letters that have changed the course of history. George Mueller prayed and hundreds of orphans were fed and clothed. Pat Robertson bought a TV station with no money, and now we have a Christian Broadcasting Network. But super-spiritual persons do nonsensical things and fall on their faces.

To be perfectly fair, I must say that most of these super-spiritual people know not what they do. There are a few psychopathic liars among Christians, to be sure, but very few. Most of us (I say *us* because I am one, too) who become caught up in super-spiritual leadings are not so much evil as stupid.

As I said before, we want to do a certain thing badly—so badly that whenever we pray, we strain to hear the voice of God saying yes to our petition. We, of course, mutter a perfunctory "not my will but thine be done," but no matter. God knows our hearts. And our hearts, being "deceitful and desperately wicked," turn our desire into God's desire.

Ways to
Avoid the Trap

What can we do then, in the face of these stupid deceitful hearts, to be sure that our leadings are really from God? Here are a few suggestions to help those with this heart trouble:

1. Do not (in spite of all I have said) try to be totally logical, determining never to be led by supernatural means. This will drive you into another trap, that of super-spiritual *logic*. It will make you dry and inflexible.

2. Check your Bible. God never leads us contrary to his Word. One of the signs of super-spiritual leading is the feeling that you are somehow a Special Case.

3. Take your leadings to your spiritual leaders. (If you do not have any, you are already too super-spiritual for this book to do you any good.) One of the jobs of spiritual leaders is to help their followers receive guidance from the Lord.

4. Give it some time. If God really wants you to do something, and you really want to do his will, it is *his* responsibility to show you how. Do not be in such a hurry to follow your first small "leading."

5. Do not tell everybody. If you do, you will feel committed to the leading and be less likely to change your mind. No one likes to be laughed at or teased with, "But I thought God told you to . . . "

6. Be suspicious of leadings that get you out of uncomfortable situations. God was and is often fond of

placing his chosen ones *into* those kinds of situations, in order to train them.

7. Finally, be willing to look back at your misfired leadings with 20/20 hindsight and say, "I was wrong. God was not saying that at all." If you do not, you will have to move from super-spiritual *leadings* to super-spiritual *lying*.

Super-Spiritual Me

Let me close with a personal anecdote. About ten years ago, when my wife and I were expecting our first child, we received what we thought was a word from the Lord. The word (or words) were "Matthew David." My wife and I were overjoyed, and we told everyone that the child would be a boy and that God had instructed us to name him Matthew David. I was excited about the boy's future, believing that he would be another Billy Graham, or at least an outstanding preacher or missionary.

But "he" was a girl—Joy Suzanne Sterner (who may yet be another Billy Graham). We were not disappointed; we loved her. But we *were* shocked, embarrassed, and properly put in our place. Two years later, Matthew David was born. We were so sure we had heard a certain thing from the Lord. And we were wrong. And so might you be.

C H A P T E R 1 4

If Only I Had More Faith

The Super-Spiritual Faith Syndrome

"There's no use trying," she said. "One can't believe impossible things."
"I daresay you haven't had much practice," said the Queen. "When I was your age, I did it for half-an-hour a day. Why, sometimes I've believed as many as six impossible things before breakfast."   —*Lewis Carroll*

"How *are* you?" The words sounded innocent enough, and the face wore a sincere "Christian caring" look, so I decided to risk an honest answer. "Not too well, really. My kids are down with the bug and my wife is starting to get it, too. I'm not quite so . . ."

Her face turned ashen, and she stepped back as if I were unclean. "Don't confess that," she shrieked. "It'll *happen* to you!"

"You don't understand," I retorted. "It *has* happened."

"No, *you* don't understand," she corrected. "If you confess positively, you can have whatever you want. If you confess this sickness, it will go on and on. God works according to his spoken word. If you don't *speak* it, you don't *get* it! Just say that they are healed and they *will* be. You need to understand what the Bible says about faith. Here! Just read this booklet by Brother ————! It will explain everything." Having thus ministered to my needs, she smiled wisely and hurried off.

Mike Yaconelli tells of a similar event in his book *Tough Faith:*

My wife and I . . . decided to visit a new church in our neighborhood. . . . The pastor was fresh from seminary and possessed an eager idealism about the future of the church.

The worship service was built around the theme of "The God of Surprises." During a time of congregational sharing, each person was to tell a recent experience which illustrated how God surprises us. . . . Soon it was my turn. I said, "Well, God surprises me by not being around when I need him, by acting the opposite of what I expect and by remaining silent when I desperately need him to say something."

As soon as the words left my mouth, I knew I had blown it. What I'd tried to say was that God acts like God, not like man. He doesn't fit into any category, and I just can't get used to God behaving like God. But that's not what the group hears. . . .

They felt it their duty to defend God . . . [and said] "I used to feel the same way" (translation: you will have no excuse, dummy, if you don't accept my answer, because it worked for me and I was exactly like you), "but then I discovered something that really changed my life." . . .

I got the message. What the lady was saying was [that] my answer was incorrect. In my opinion, that's why people with questions feel uncomfortable in church.

Stories like this would be comical if they were not so common. Unfortunately, they represent the lunatic fringe of a very popular form of super-spirituality—the *super-spiritual faith syndrome.* This neurosis comes in two forms—both guaranteed to make you miserable. The *negative* type, a form of "I'm just awful," will make you hate yourself. The *positive* kind, "If you only had more faith, like me," will make everybody hate you. You can pick the one that suits your personality, or use both, depending upon how you feel at the time.

What's Wrong with Positive Thinking?

Super-spiritual faith, otherwise known as "right thinking," "positive confession," or "having the authority of a true believer," is usually professed by Christians with good health, few major problems, and lots of money. It is a philosophy which believes that if one says a thing often enough, it will (nay, it *must)* come true. If I feel sick, I must never say, "I feel sick." I must say instead, "Jesus has already healed me and I feel fine." If I am broke, I should say something like, "God is prospering me and has already met all my needs," over and over. (This is somewhat like that word Great! you learned in chapter 5.)

Proponents of this philosophy write things like this:

You can always tell if a person's believing is right by what he says. If his confession is wrong, his believing is wrong. If his believing is wrong, his thinking is wrong. If his thinking is wrong, it's because his mind has not been renewed with the Word of God. . . . Don't confess your doubts. You don't have any more business with doubt than you have with dope. It's of the devil. Doubt is contraband goods. Doubt is just as evil as dope, and if it's evil we haven't got any business with it. . . . When you confess your doubts, fears, weakness, and disease, you are openly confessing that God's Word is not true. (Kenneth Hagan, *Right and Wrong Thinking for Christians)*

Now, I would like to believe that, wouldn't you? Anyone with sense would like to have all his diseases healed, his bank account grow, his children get into Harvard Law School, and his car run 362 miles on a gallon of regular. I am not questioning the sincerity of those who believe this philosophy. They are, for the most part, earnest men and women who have a great desire to help people. But I object to their program of 100 percent good things from God, for two reasons: First, it does not harmonize with the Scriptures; second, it does not work.

Why Was Paul Sick?

If everyone is supposed to be healthy, rich, and free from all problems, why was Paul sick? "You know that it was because of a bodily illness that I preached the gospel to you the first time" (Gal. 4:13 NAS). Why did he leave Trophimus sick at Miletus? (II Tim. 4:20). Why did he advise Timothy to "take a little [wine] sometimes as medicine for your stomach because you are sick so often"? (I Tim. 5:23 TLB).

It would seem to me that if Paul had been as "spiritual" as these new teachers of faith are, he would have advised Timothy to "confess healing for your stomach." Instead, he actually makes a (gasp) negative confession. According to the super-spiritual faith preachers, this can only mean that he had a lack of faith, or that he knew Timothy did. But Paul claims that Timothy had made a "good profession before many witnesses" (I Tim. 6:12). It certainly is puzzling, isn't it?

Then there is Paul's "thorn in the flesh." Now, we do not *know* that it was a physical ailment. It may have been a harrassment from Satan, or he may have been bugged by some people who followed him around (most commentaries think, however, that it *was* physical). Nevertheless, Paul did *not* respond to the problem by claiming that it was not there. Three times, he *asked* God to remove it. He did not demand, claim, or assert any "authority of a believer." He *asked!* And God said no.

Why Was Jesus Poor?

If God wants us to be rich, why was Jesus poor? "The Son of man has nowhere to lay His head" (Matt. 8:20 NAS). Why would Jesus say something like this—"Woe unto you that are rich! . . . Woe unto you that are full!"—if he wants us to be affluent (Luke 6:24-25)? If the Bible *wants* us to have lucre, why does it call it "filthy"? I agree that Scripture teaches us that the root of evil is not money itself, but the love of it (I Tim. 6:10). But look up the words *rich* and *riches* in a concordance and see what the Bible thinks about rich men and their money.

Look here, you rich men, now is the time to cry and groan with anguished grief because of all the terrible troubles ahead of you. Your wealth is even now rotting away, and your fine clothes are becoming mere moth-eaten rags. The value of your gold and silver is dropping fast, yet it will stand as evidence against you, and eat your flesh like fire. That is what you have stored up for yourselves, to receive on that coming day of judgment. . . . You have spent your years here on earth having fun, satisfying your every whim, and now your fat hearts are ready for the slaughter. (James 5:1-6 TLB)

Why So Many Thorns?

If God wants our life to be a bed of roses, why does his Word promise so many thorns? "Dear friends, don't be bewildered or surprised when you go through the fiery trials ahead, for this is no strange, unusual thing that is going to happen to you. Instead, be really glad—because these trials will make you partners with Christ in his suffering" (I Pet. 4:12-13 TLB).

Jesus promises us that we will be hated and persecuted (John 15:18-25). The disciples, after being beaten, rejoiced that they had been found worthy to suffer (Acts 5:41). Paul wants to know Jesus "and the power of his resurrection, and the fellowship of his sufferings, being made conformable unto his death" (Phil. 3:10). Peter says that we should follow the example of Christ and suffer as he did (I Pet. 2:21).

The Swinging of the Pendulum

Where does all the weird teaching come from? It comes from the natural swing of the pendulum away from the former super-spirituality—that it is somehow godly to be sick, poor, and in misery. For years, the church taught that if God really liked you, you would be smitten with all kinds of pain. It was spiritual to suffer. But the Bible does not teach that it is spiritual to suffer. It teaches that it is spiritual to suffer *in a Christlike manner*, just as it is spiritual to be prosperous in a Christlike manner.

Acting on such Scripture passages as "abundant life," "prospering as your soul prospereth," and "righteousness, peace and joy in the Holy Ghost," these new teachers have happily abandoned the old super-spiritual suffering. And good riddance! They have found the other side of the coin!

The problem is that now they see *only* the other side of the coin. They preach healing, joy, prosperity, and the good life. So does the Bible. But the Bible *also* preaches death, sadness, poverty, and suffering. We are not *necessarily* spiritual, either way. We are spiritual only if we handle in a godly manner whatever God gives us.

What's Wrong with Me?

Most of us are not in the same ball park with the super-spiritual positive-faith preachers. We know from our own experience that it just does not work for us. (I believed this positive-confession stuff for two whole weeks, during which time my business collapsed and I caught a cold.) For us, then, there is the traditional negative-faith game—"If only I had more faith."

It works like this. Whenever you or one of your family is sick, depressed, or worried about something, do the following: Make a face like the man in the pain-killer commercial (the one who has not yet taken the pain-killer), groan and say, "This wouldn't have happened to me if only I had had more faith." If this fails to make you miserable, beat your breast and add, "The

Lord is punishing me for my secret sins." Never explain
what your secret sins *are*. This would spoil the game by
allowing you to repent and be forgiven of them.

Always assume that no one else *ever* has had any of
these problems. After all, you never hear anyone *talk*
about them, so you must be the only one. After all, you *do*
doubt, don't you? And if you doubt, you must not have
any faith, right? And do not worry if you are not able to
work up a lot of guilt all by yourself. Soon someone will
come along and help you.

With Friends
Like Job's—
Who Needs Satan?

The Super-spiritual faith people claim that Job got what
he deserved. He simply did not have the faith necessary
to forestall his troubles. After all, did he not admit that
"what I always feared has happened to me"? (Job 3:25
TLB). "Fear is negative faith," they claim. "Job made a
negative confession and reaped the results." They
should listen to what *God* had to say about Job: "Have
you noticed my servant Job? He is the finest man in all the
earth—a good man who fears God and will have nothing
to do with evil" (1:8 TLB). God bragged about Job to
Satan. Could he say the same about you or me?

But here to comfort and console Job come his three
friends. To their credit, for seven days and nights they
kept their mouths shut, since they saw that his suffering
was too great for words. We could learn a great deal
about ministering to those in grief from their example.

When Job began to vent his anger and frustration,
however, it was too much for his friends. Feeling that
their appointed mission in life was to defend the honor of
God, they explained to Job why he was suffering. "You
must have sinned, Job. I mean, have you ever known an
innocent man to have troubles like these? Our advice to

you is to go and confess your sins before it's too late. You must have forgotten God. *You need more faith!"* (Sterner Version).

So when all the talk was over (it goes on for more than thirty chapters), and the Lord speaks to them, what did he say? "I am angry with you [Eliphaz] and with your two friends, for you have not been right in what you have said about me, *as my servant Job was.* Now . . . offer a burnt offering for yourselves; and my servant Job will pray for you, and I will accept his prayer on your behalf, and won't destroy you as I should because of your sin, your failure to speak rightly concerning my servant Job" (42:7-8 TLB, italics added).

Trying to Figure God Out

Job's friends should have listened to what *God* had to say about him. Because they did not, they almost lost their lives. When you see someone in a jam, stop and think before you assume a lack of faith or some secret sin. Perhaps God is using that person in a way of his own. Perhaps the reasons for the sickness, financial difficulties, or other problems are beyond your comprehension. Perhaps God thinks it is none of your business.

The problem with the super-spiritual faith group (positive *and* negative) is that they think it is necessary to understand God. "God left us a Book," they reason. "So if we study it long enough, we ought to be able to predict his ways." But theology is not a predictive science. The Bible is not a textbook, and God's ways are "past finding out."

"How impossible it is for us to understand his decisions and his methods! For who among us can know the mind of the Lord? Who knows enough to be his counselor and guide? And who could ever offer to the Lord enough to induce him to act?" (Rom. 11:33*b*-35

TLB). "For my thoughts are not your thoughts, neither are your ways my ways, saith the Lord" (Isa. 55:8).

What is the point, you might ask, of being able to understand God—to persuade him to do what you want; to predict him; to put him in a comfortable box. Knowledge is power. But God is not some kind of cosmic bellhop. He is the King of kings, the great I Am, the Lord of the universe! And he does *not* have to answer to *us!*

Now, Faith Is . . .

So, what *is* faith? After all, our Lord *did* heal people because they had faith. Matthew tells us that Jesus was ineffective in his hometown because of the unbelief of the people there (Matt. 13:58). Obviously, if we have faith, it helps, and if we do not believe, it hurts. Let us turn to the super-spiritual's favorite Scripture, Hebrews, chapter eleven: "Now faith is the assurance of things hoped for, the conviction of things not seen. For by it the men of old gained approval. . . . And without faith it is impossible to please Him, for he who comes to God must believe that He is, and that He is a rewarder of those who seek Him" (1-2, 6 NAS).

So to have faith is to be sure of things that we do not yet see—to believe the promises of God. We need faith to "gain approval"—to please him. But what *kind* of faith? We need simply to believe that he exists and that he will reward us for looking for him.

"By faith Abraham, when he was called, obeyed by going out . . . *not knowing where he was going* (11:8 NAS, italics added). This is the key verse. If Abraham had known where he was going, his action would not have been based on faith. If you or I *know* we are going to be healed or delivered from a certain problem, our belief *is not faith.*

Faith does not consist of magical incantations guaranteed to move the hand of the Almighty. Faith is the abandonment of ourselves to the good and perfect will of God when we do not know where we are going. "Our Lord in Gethsemane made a petitionary prayer," declares C. S. Lewis, "and did not get what He asked for." "Thy will be done" is the bottom line of all faith.

Does Faith Eliminate Problems?

Is all doubt bad? James says that we must ask without any doubt, or we will become "double minded" and unstable in all our ways (James 1:5-8). But James is talking about asking God for wisdom, not about asking for deliverance from personal problems. "By faith even Sarah herself received ability to conceive, even beyond the proper time of life, since she considered Him faithful who had promised" (Heb. 11:11 NAS).

Sarah? Are you kidding? Don't you remember her reaction to the Lord's message that she would have a baby? "Sarah laughed silently. 'A woman my age have a baby?' she scoffed to herself. 'And with a husband as old as mine?'" (Gen. 18:12 TLB). Then when God asked Abraham why Sarah laughed, she denied that she had. "'I didn't laugh,' she lied, for she was afraid" (Gen. 18:15 TLB). This is faith? *Yes!*

I think that faith means obedience to the will of God, whether we understand that will or not. Perhaps Thomas had more faith than the other disciples. He followed Jesus even when he thought they all would die. God's promises *are* hard for us to believe when someone we know is dying. But perhaps Job had the greatest faith of all. "Though he slay me, yet will I trust in him" (Job 13:15).

Like Sarah, I want to cover up my lack of faith, for I too am afraid. I want to believe; I do not want to doubt. I want to be a great hero of the faith. Or do I? There is one part of chapter eleven that I never have heard the super-spiritual faith preachers quote—the last part. After telling the glorious deeds of Daniel, David, Samuel, and the prophets, the writer of Hebrews tells about those who

experienced mockings and scourgings, yes, also chains and imprisonment. They were stoned, they were sawn in two, they were tempted, they were put to death with the sword; they went about in sheepskins, in goatskins, being destitute, afflicted, ill-treated (men of whom the world was not worthy), wandering in deserts and mountains and caves and holes in the ground. And all these, having gained approval through their faith, did not receive what was promised. (Hebrews 11:36-39 NAS)

The next time you ask God to increase your faith, you had better step back!

What About the Rest of the World?

I would like to see these brothers take their super-spiritual faith to Bangladesh, Cambodia, or Calcutta. It is easy to believe that God wants us to be rich and healthy when we live in the richest and healthiest country in the world. To my mind, this philosophy fosters a smug self-centeredness that refuses to care about the rest of the world. After all, if those starving Cambodians just had more faith, they wouldn't be in that fix, right?

I do not know why there are widows and orphans in God's world. I *do* know that he insists that I take care of them. It seems to me that a super-spiritual faith is likely to be the kind without works, described by James: "If a brother or sister is without clothing and in need of daily food, and one of you says to them, 'Go in peace, be warm and be filled,' and yet you do not give them what is necessary for their body, what use is that? Even faith, if it has no works, is dead" (James 2:15-17 NAS).

I do not know why people starve or why earthquakes destroy lives. I do not know why some sick people die and others are healed. I *do* know that there is a loving God, running the universe as he sees fit. His ways are not mine, and praise God they are not! It is not my job to demand from him or to understand him. It is my job to come humbly before him and say, "Lord, I believe; help thou mine unbelief" (Mark 9:24).

C H A P T E R   1 5

What Is Spiritual?

Super-Spiritual Spirituality

Where the Spirit of the Lord is, there is liberty.
—Paul (II Cor. 3:17)

Spiritual . . . 1. of, relating to, or consisting of spirit *(Webster's New Collegiate Dictionary)*.

Since I intend to devote so many pages to criticism of counterfeit spirituality *(the quality or state of pretending to be spiritual)*, I feel obliged to take some time to deal with the real thing. I do not propose to show you how to *be* spiritual (heaven knows there are already enough books about *that*). But at least you will know what it *is* . . . I think.

A Popular
Word

Nearly eight hundred times, the Bible uses the word *spirit*. In both Hebrew and Greek, the words translated *spirit* mean *wind* or *breath*. A close examination reveals that the same words are used to refer to the Holy Spirit; the emotional center and life force of a person; and angels, demons, and ghosts. For our purposes, *Spirit* will refer only to the third person of the Trinity.

We are instructed in the Scriptures that we are to be very well acquainted with the Holy Spirit. We are to be born of the Spirit, be quickened and sealed with the Spirit. The Bible demands that we worship in the Spirit, stand fast in the Spirit, serve, walk after, be led by, and be holy in the Spirit.

We are to receive the Spirit, be fervent in the Spirit, glorify God and be strengthened by and renewed in the Spirit. We can have gifts and fruit of the Spirit. We can pray and sing with the Spirit. We can have fellowship with the Spirit and know the Spirit's mind. In short, we are to be "filled with the Spirit."

We also can sin against the Holy Spirit. We can lie to, tempt, grieve, and ultimately quench the Spirit. The story of Ananias and Sapphira is a famous example (Acts 5). That couple pretended to be big-time givers. Having sold some property, they claimed they were giving *all* the money to the apostles, but Peter knew better.

"Ananias," said Peter, "why has Satan filled your heart to lie to the Holy Spirit? . . . You have not lied to men, but to God" (Acts 5:3-4 RSV). And Ananias (and later his wife) promptly fell down dead. "Everybody tells me they want a New Testament Church," says my friend Ward Williams, "but nobody wants *that* part." Interesting, isn't it, that the only case of this type of miracle is found in connection with the sin of hypocrisy?

What Is the Spirit For?

Just what *is* the purpose, the ministry, of the Holy Spirit? What does the Spirit do? Jesus explained it in chapters fourteen and sixteen of the Gospel of John. Let me quote a few verses:

I will ask the Father, and he will give you another Counselor to be with you forever—the Spirit of truth . . . will be in you. . . . The Holy Spirit, whom the Father will send in my name, will teach you all things and will remind you of everything I have said to you. . . . When he comes, he will convict the world of guilt in regard to sin and righteousness and judgment. . . . He will guide you into all truth. . . . He will bring glory to me by taking from what is mine and making it known to you. (14:16-17, 26; 16:8, 13, 14 NIV)

Jesus was speaking to a grief-smitten group of disciples. They were just coming to grips with the fact that he really *was* going to die and leave them. "But I won't leave you alone, guys," he promised. "I'll send you someone to take my place, to teach you and comfort you. In fact, though you probably find this incredible, it really is going to be good for you that I'm leaving and he's coming" (Sterner Version).

Spiritual = Me + Spirit

So we are to receive and be led by the Spirit, in order to work the works of Christ in the world. Jesus is gone, at least in body. Only he really is not, because the Holy Spirit energizes Christians to work together to accomplish Christ's purposes in the world. This, interestingly enough, is called the Body of Christ. He is still here as long as you and I are spiritual.

"The meaning of being spiritual is to belong to the Holy Spirit," writes Watchman Nee in *The Spiritual Man*. "Obedience to the Holy Spirit makes one a spiritual believer. No word does he speak nor act does he perform according to himself; rather does he deny his natural power each in order to draw power from the spirit. In a word, a spiritual man lives by the spirit."

But what does this spiritual person look like? How is he or she different from an unspiritual person? Some say the difference is a matter of prayer and personal devotions. Some say it is fasting. Others claim that to be really spiritual, one must have had a certain observable experience. Still others point to the things one must or must not do—a large traditional set of rules, which varies from church to church. Most of these people have one thing in common. They are copying someone else.

When I became a Christian, I was sure of two things. One, I was supposed to be spiritual. Two, I was not spiritual. So I began to look around at people who were, and when I found some, I copied them. Now this was not so bad for awhile, because I *did* pick up a good many worthwhile habits, such as going to prayer meeting and reading spiritual literature. But after awhile, I began to seem so much like bits and pieces of every "spiritual giant" I knew that no one could find *me* anymore.

Of course, after some time, I discovered the hard truth. My spiritual giants had feet of clay. Hanging around them night and day gave me an opportunity to see them as real people. (I must, in all fairness, point out that most of them were not trying to be spiritual giants at all. I had a need to see them as something they were not.) So I found new heroes to copy—the writers of devotional books.

I began to aspire to the prayer life of Martin Luther (for two or three hours before breakfast). I wanted to be disciplined like John Wesley, to have the faith of George Mueller, and to "practice the presence of God" like Brother Lawrence. I wanted to win souls like John Hyde and pray for healing like Smith Wigglesworth, or at least like Katherine Kuhlman. In addition, I coveted the intelligence of C. S. Lewis, the openness and honesty of Keith Miller, and the humor of Charlie Shedd.

Real People?

Then a terrible thing happened! I found out (from his own book) that one of my biggest heroes was just a lowly human being like the rest of us. Dave Wilkerson had confessed to being mad at God, afraid of airplanes, and to almost leaving his wife. I was shocked! I was horrified! I mean, he wrote books and everything. He was on TV and spoke at big conventions. He couldn't do this to me!

Then I began to do research, and sure enough, I found some more awful truths. *All* those people in books are human! Did you know that John Wesley could not get along with his wife? That the apostle Paul, too, had trouble getting along with people? And that Martin Luther could get along with almost nobody? I mean, if I looked closely enough, I probably could find out something bad about Charlie Shedd!

Slowly, ever so slowly, the Lord began to pound the truth into my thick skull. "I don't want another Luther, Kuhlman, or Shedd; I want my Spirit to energize John Sterner."

"But Lord," I whined, "how will I know what to do if I don't copy somebody? What measurement will I use to determine my spirituality? I need to know how to tell when I have arrived!"

"Don't worry about it," the answer seemed to come. "*I'll* know."

A Fruit Inspection

The only place I know that clearly gives us some measurement of spirituality is the fifth chapter of Galatians. "The fruit of the Spirit is love, joy, peace, patience, kindness, goodness, faithfulness, gentleness and self-control" (Gal. 5:22 NIV). But is my joy exactly like your joy? Are we called to be patient about the same things?

Interestingly enough, the chapter begins like this: "It is for freedom that Christ has set us free. Stand firm then, and do not let yourselves be burdened again by a yoke of slavery." Paul was enraged by the thought that a group of Jews wanted the Gentile Christians to be circumcised (so that they would be "like everybody else"—in this case, the Jews). He writes, "If you let yourself be circumcised, Christ will be of no value to you at all. . . .

For in Christ Jesus neither circumcision nor uncircumcision has any value. The only thing that counts is faith expressing itself through love" (Gal. 5:2, 6 NIV).

But should not my faith and yours express themselves similarly, if they both are expressing themselves through love? Yes, similarly—but not exactly. It was God who gave the commandment of circumcision to Abraham. Yet it also was God who inspired the council in Jerusalem to revoke that commandment for the Gentile believers. It was decided that what had been good for God's people for thousands of years was not good for his new people. And what is good for you may not be good for me. Declares C. S. Lewis:

It takes all sorts to make a world. Or even a church. This may be even truer of a church. If grace perfects nature it must expand all our natures into the full richness of the diversity which God intended when He made them, and Heaven will display far more variety than Hell. "One fold" doesn't mean "one pool." Cultivated roses and daffodils are no more alike than wild roses and daffodils. . . . I don't doubt, then, that Rose's method was the right one for her. It wouldn't be for me, any more than for you . . . "Who art thou that judgest Another's servant?" *(The Weight of Glory)*

Different Strokes for Different Folks

It always has intrigued me that Jesus included both a Zealot and a tax collector in his inner circle of friends. I wonder if he had them bunk together on trips. Of all the Jews at that time, no two would have had more natural hatred for each other. (A Zealot was fanatically opposed to Rome, while a tax collector worked for Rome.) You do not see this diversity in the Pharisees. They were all alike, stamped out of the same dreary mold. They all prayed the same way, preached the same way, rigorously followed the same rules. There are no Pharisees anymore, but there surely are a lot of people who follow Jesus. I hope they all never try to do it the same way.

You see, God the Holy Spirit never changes. Each man and woman is different, and *we are supposed to be different.* We were created that way. Not only that, but the Spirit gives each of us different gifts and ministries with which to serve God and one another. "Is everyone an apostle? Of course not. Is everyone a preacher? No. Are all teachers? Does everyone have the power to do miracles? Can everyone heal the sick? Of course not" (I Cor. 12:29-30 TLB).

One night our Bible study group counted thirty-two different gifts and ministries given by the Holy Spirit. "Now here is what I am trying to say: All of you together are the one body of Christ and each one of you is a separate and necessary part of it" (I Cor. 12:27 TLB). (You can find several of these gifts and ministries listed in Romans 12, Ephesians 4, and I Corinthians 12.)

John's Infallible Rules for Spirituality

Having said (and quoted) all this, I will now set forth *my* views on the process of becoming spiritual. I do so with fear and trembling, because I know that some of you will set these views in stone and thereby inhibit your spiritual growth. On the other hand, some of you may be helped to find your own views by looking at mine.

First, becoming spiritual is a process, rather than an event. Paul told the believers in Corinth that they were not yet spiritual enough to be fed meat, because they were still baby Christians. (The proof of this, according to I Corinthians 3, is that they argued so much.) Peter admonishes us to "grow in grace." Jesus compares us to the branches of a vine (he being the vine). Slowly we mature, take in sunlight and water, and finally produce fruit.

Second, becoming spiritual is hard work. Paul compares it to running a race, fighting a war, or farming the land.

Imagine how difficult it was to plow with oxen, how much an Olympic runner must train, and what it must have been like to wage a war with swords and axes.

Third, becoming spiritual is a never-ending journey. We are always becoming—never arriving. Until we reach heaven (which some see as the beginning of yet another never-ending journey), we are never fully spiritual. This does not mean that we are not *truly* spiritual—it just means that we never are quite past the point where this treasure of the Holy Spirit is contained in "earthen vessels" (II Cor. 4:7).

Fourth, as far as the activities of man are concerned, they are not labeled secular or sacred—spiritual versus unspiritual. Everything that is motivated by the Spirit is spiritual. "[God] can have no standing as a department," continues C. S. Lewis. "Either He is an illusion or else our whole life falls under Him. We have no non-religious activities; only religious and irreligious."

Whether an activity is religious, or spiritual, depends upon its motivation. Thus I can play softball spiritually and sing hymns unspiritually. I can write an irreligious sermon or a religious joke. I can be secular when I lead someone to Christ and sacred when I have sex. "In him we live and move and have our being." God does not want us to abdicate the human race in order to become spiritual. He wants us to be led by his Spirit in all things.

I am neither good nor bad, I am both . . .
I am neither guilty nor innocent, I am both . . .
I am neither loving nor hateful, I am both . . .
I am neither pure nor impure, I am both;
and because God accepts me, I will accept myself.
　　　　　　　—Cecil Osborne, *You're in Charge*

Fifth, no one's spirituality is exactly like that of anyone else. Both you and I may be very spiritual, but be exact opposites. One of my colleagues attempts to pray for hours in the early morning. I sleep in the early morning. He likes to fast and read books by medieval mystics; I prefer to eat and read Erma Bombeck. Each of us does his own thing to the glory of God.

Sixth, the more spiritual we become, the less people will understand us. A "fanatic" is anyone who loves Jesus more than I do. Moses was misunderstood. So were Elijah, David, and Jeremiah, to name a few. Some religious folk thought Jesus was possessed of a demon. Stephen, Peter, and Paul all were criticized by their contemporaries. "A man's foes shall be they of his own household," promised our Lord.

Some Spiritual Words

Let me conclude this chapter with some words from a more spiritual one: Romans, chapter eight, in which the words *spirit* and *spiritual* are mentioned twenty-two times.

There is therefore now no condemnation to them which are in Christ Jesus, who walk not after the flesh, but after the Spirit. For the law of the Spirit . . . hath made me free from the law of sin . . . that the righteousness of the law might be fulfilled in us, who walk . . . after the Spirit. (1-4)

But ye are not in the flesh, but in the Spirit, if so be that the Spirit of God dwell in you. . . . And if Christ be in you . . . the Spirit is life. (9-10)

For ye have not received the spirit of bondage again to fear; but ye have received the Spirit of adoption, whereby we cry, Abba, Father. The Spirit itself beareth witness with our Spirit, that we are the children of God. And if children, then heirs; heirs of God, and joint-heirs with Christ. (15-17)

C H A P T E R   1 6

How Did I Get Like This?

The Way to Become Super-Spiritual

"Contrariwise," continued Tweedledee, *"if it was so, it might be; and if it were so, it would be; but as it isn't, it ain't. That's logic."*   —*Lewis Carroll*

As I reflect upon the preceding chapters, I am reminded of a cartoon that showed a man gazing in wonder upon a very complicated map. "You are here," read the caption below an X. Above another X, the caption read, "You *should* be here." I can just imagine the man wondering to himself, "How the devil did I get here? Is it even *possible* to get where I should be?"

"I love your book," said a friend, "but I hate it, too. I'm *in* it." Well, so am I. And so, perhaps, are you. So far, so good—exposing the problem is the easy part. The hard part is to find out what to *do* about it. It is easy for me to preach to my congregation for hours about their awful sins, but where do they go from there?

In order to change, the first step is to retrace the steps that brought us to super-spirituality in the first place. If we can discover how we got here, maybe we *can* get to where we "should" be. So, with many apologies for oversimplification, here goes.

The Gospel According to Freud—
I Was Born This Way

Sigmund Freud was to psychology what Einstein was to mathematics—he turned the whole subject upside down. He discovered that a person finds direction in life by utilizing subconscious, as well as conscious motives. Freud searched for these motives in the early childhood of the patient. He concluded that the motives are largely sexual in nature and that they are hooked to biologically determined stages of growth. In other words, the way human beings find meaning is instinctual. Our problems, Freud declared, start when some part of society (usually the parents) interferes with the natural process. We become inhibited, stunted in our growth, unable to be free. His method of counseling was to encourage the "id" (that part of us that wants to be free and natural) to break free from the "superego" (that part of us that says, "You shouldn't do that").

All very well. But what happens if my superego is telling my id not to beat my wife, or that I should not rob the First Savings and Loan? Do I really want to silence my conscience? At any rate, Freud's theories have been passed down to the common people in the form of "You can't help it. You were born that way." A modern folksong by Anna Russell describes it this way:

I went to my psychiatrist to be psychoanalysed,
To find out why I killed the cat and blacked my husband's eyes.
He laid me on a downy couch to see what he could find,
And this is what he dredged up from my subconscious mind. . . .

When I was one, my mummy hid my dolly in a trunk
And so it follows naturally that I am always drunk.
When I was two I saw my father kiss the maid one day,
And that is why I suffer now from kleptoman-i-ay! . . .

At three I had a feeling of ambivalence towards my brothers,
And so it follows naturally I poison all my lovers,
But I am happy now I've learned the lesson this has taught,
That everything I do that's wrong is someone else's fault!

117

The Gospel According to Skinner— Society Did It to Me

While Freud put his patients on the couch, another group of psychologists ran rats through mazes. Today this group is headed by Dr. B. F. Skinner and is influencing our educational system with "behavior modification."

Skinner believes that a person's actions are dependent entirely upon the rewards and punishments brought to bear by others. If I can find out what a person wants and does not want, I can persuade him to do anything. Since our society rewards certain behaviors and punishes others, one really is not responsible for the things one does. If we want better people, we must change society through education.

Psychologists have been arguing for years about the relative importance of heredity and environment. The message that comes through to the common people, though, is this: No one ever is to be held morally responsible for his actions. (In all fairness I must say that most psychologists do not act as if this were true.)

The Gospel According to Humanism— Choose Your Destiny

For the past thirty years, another group of psychologists, a third force as they are sometimes called, has taught a different message. Led by such men as Carl Rogers, Abraham Maslow, Fritz Perls, and Albert Ellis, this group disclaims most of the earlier dogmas. "Men are free to choose their own paths," claim these humanistic psychologists, "and if this freedom is pointed out, they usually will choose what is right." (*Right*, of course, is defined by whoever is using the word.)

The humanists are influenced by the philosophy of existentialism—that the only real meaning of life is the meaning a person gives to it. They encourage group encounters, values clarification, living "in the now," and intimate interpersonal relationships. Their influence is being felt in the church in the form of "relational theology."

As Shakespeare said, "Confusion now has made his masterpiece." Who is right and who is wrong? All of the above. And none of the above. They all are somewhat correct, and they all are most definitely incomplete in their assessment of the human dilemma.

The Gospel According to God— I Sinned

"In Adam's fall, we sinned all," reads the *New England Primer.* "The heart is deceitful above all things and desperately wicked," preached the prophet Jeremiah. "Who can know it?" (17:9). Paul agrees: "There is none righteous, no not one . . . there is none that doeth good . . . all have sinned and come short of the glory of God" (Rom. 3:10, 12, 23). The fly in the psychological ointment, which Freud, Skinner, and others failed to take into consideration, is the enormity, the totality, of sin in the world.

There is nothing in this world that is not tainted with the results of the fall of the human race. Giving credit where it is due, I must say that when Adam and Eve sinned, they did a thorough job. My heredity is sinful, my society is sinful, and thus my choices will be sinful.

How many times have you heard that someone was a chip off the old block? In many ways, some of which I refuse to admit even to myself, I *am* just like my dad. One important similarity I recognize is that my dad and I both are sinners, as were his father and grandfather, and all before them.

"You mean that little innocent babies are born sinful?" Yes, I mean exactly that. What do little innocent babies

119

want? They want to be held, fed, played with, and changed. They want their whole world to hold them as the center of attention. They want their own way. And they are very vocal about getting it. In short, like the rest of humanity, little innocent babies are very selfish.

So Freud was right. I *was* born that way. "Behold," says David. "I was shapen in iniquity; and in sin did my mother conceive me" (Ps. 51:5). "Therefore, just as sin entered the world through one man, and death through sin . . . in this way death came to all men, because all sinned. . . . Death reigned from the time of Adam to the time of Moses" (Rom. 5:12-14 NIV).

Sounds pretty grim, doesn't it? It would be, too, if Paul had stopped there. But he went on to state that we who receive God's gift of grace and righteousness can overcome our defect of birth. So Freud was wrong, too. I may have been born this way, but I do not need to stay this way.

Society and the "Shoulds"

Fritz Perls, the founder of Gestalt therapy, has this to say about our environment:

Most therapies try to adjust the person to society. That was not too bad . . . when society was stable, but now with the rapid changes going on it is more difficult. . . . Also more people are not willing to adjust. . . . They think society stinks. . . . I consider that the basic personality of our time is neurotic. . . . I believe we are living in an insane society, and that you have only the choice of participating in collective psychosis or . . . becom[ing] healthy and perhaps also crucified. (*Gestalt Therapy Verbatim*)

How does society modify our behavior? Through the rewards and punishments of approval and disapproval. You are a good little boy/girl *if* you do/think/say/believe/want/act like your mommy/daddy/friends/country/

school/church/TV/magazine says you *should!* And you are a bad/sinful/unpatriotic/disgusting/uncool/not-with-the-program little boy/girl/creep/nerd/monster/jerk/student/parishioner if you do not do what they all say you should. Karen Horney describes this as "the tyranny of the shoulds."

He should be the utmost of honesty, generosity, considerateness, justice, dignity, courage, unselfishness. He should be the perfect lover, husband, teacher. He should be able to endure everything. He should like everybody. He should love his parents, his wife, his country; or he should not be attached to any thing or anybody, nothing or nobody, nothing should matter to him, he should never feel hurt, and he should always be serene, unruffled. He should always enjoy life; or he should be above pleasure and enjoyment. He should be spontaneous; he should always control his feelings. He should know, understand and foresee everything. He should be able to solve every problem of his own or of others in no time. He should be able to overcome every difficulty of his as soon as he sees it. He should never be tired or fall ill. He should always be able to find a job. He should be able to do things in one hour which can only be done in two to three hours. *(Neurosis and Human Growth)*

"I'm certain you are familiar with this game," Perls goes on. "One part of you talks to the other part and says, 'You should be better, you should not be this way, you should not do this, you shouldn't be what you are, you should be what you are not!'" Perls' solution, as well as that of many other psychologists, is to drop *all* shoulds and do what we want. This is sometimes a compelling idea, but it does not square very well with denying oneself, taking up the cross, and following Jesus.

Jesus Was Different

On the other hand, our Lord did not seem to mind being different from the crowd. "How come?" asked the Pharisees, John's followers, and even the Twelve. "How come you don't fast as we do, obey the sabbath rules as we do, wash your hands as we do? Why do you touch lepers, hang around with whores, and teach in riddles? Why won't you be like we think you should be, Jesus?" The Pharisees had an answer. "He has a demon; he is possessed by Beelzebul." Even his family worried about him. "He is out of his mind," they said (Mark 3:21 NIV). But some knew that he was "the Christ, the son of the living God" and that *he had the authority to make his own shoulds.*

So Skinner was right. Society *does* shape us. And curiously enough, both the Bible and the psychologists agree that society shapes us very badly. Skinner says that we cannot help it, that we are merely helpless pawns in a game of invincible forces. But Jesus beat those forces and calls us to do the same. "If the Son sets you free, you will be free indeed" (John 8:36 NIV).

The Challenge of the Choices

In the beginning [writes Barry Stevens] was I, and I was good.

Then came the Other I. Outside authority. This was confusing. And then Other I became *very* confused because there were so many *different* outside authorities.

Sit nicely. Leave the room to blow your nose. Don't do that, that's silly. Why the poor child doesn't even know how to pick a bone! Flush the toilet at night because if you don't it makes it harder to clean. *Don't flush the toilet at night*—you wake people up! Always be nice to people, even if you don't like them; you mustn't hurt their feelings. Be frank and honest. If you don't tell people what you think of them, that's cowardly. Butter knives. It is important to use butter knives. Butter knives. What foolishness! Speak nicely. Sissy! Kipling is wonderful! Ugh! Kipling!

The most important thing is to have a career. The most important thing is to get married. The heck with everyone. Be nice to everyone. The most important thing is to have sex. The most important thing is to have money in the bank. The most important thing is to have everybody like you. The most important thing is to dress well. The most important thing is to be sophisticated and to say what you don't mean and don't let anyone know how you feel. The most important thing is a black seal coat and silver and china. The most important thing is to be clean. The most important thing is to pay your debts. The most important thing is not to be taken in by anybody else. The most important thing is to love your parents. The most important thing is to work. The most important thing is to be independent. The most important thing is to speak correct English. The most important thing is to be dutiful to your husband. The most important thing is to see that your children behave well. The most important thing is to go to the right plays and read the right books. The most important thing is to do what others say. And others say *all* these things. (Barry Stevens and Carl Rogers, *Person to Person: The Problem of Being*)

Clearly, I have much to be set free from. My heritage is sinful, my society is sinful—therefore my choices will be sinful. To simply escape all the shoulds and do as I please will lead me into chaos and my society into anarchy.

Some of the saddest words in the Bible are at the end of the book of Judges. After describing throughout twenty-one chapters the lust, intrigue, murder, and corruption in Israel at that time, the writer concludes, "In those days there was no king in Israel: every man did that which was right in his own eyes."

Freedom to Serve

My freedom, then, is not a chance to do my own thing. It is rather an opportunity to do *God's* thing for me. "Freedom," says Bill Gothard, "is not the opportunity to do what we want, but the power to do what we ought [should]." And most important, it is not Mom, Dad, society, or even I who decides what I should do; it is God who must decide what I should do. And he likes me. And he wants the best for me. And he *knows* what that best thing *is*.

So all I gotta do is (1) change my heritage, (2) change my society, and (3) change my choices, and everything will be OK, right? (Of course, right!) But how?

C H A P T E R   1 7

Changing My Heredity

O Father!—chiefly known to me by Thy rod—mortal or
immortal here I die.   —*Herman Melville*

One thing the psychologists, philosophers, theologians, and ancient writers seem to agree upon is that parents are responsible to some degree for the problems of children. Euripides, four hundred years before Christ, declared that "the gods visit the sins of the fathers upon the children." Solomon admonished parents to "train up a child in the way he should go: and when he is old, he will not depart from it" (Prov. 22:6).

Any glance at the "parenting" section in bookstores (religious or secular) will confirm that this view prevails. The prominent psychologist Harry Stack Sullivan claims that providing children with good experiences will produce good attitudes, and bad experiences will produce bad attitudes. "Malevolent development," says he, "is obviously a failure of the parents to discharge their social responsibility to produce a well-behaved, well-socialized person."

All well and good, if I want to be a better parent. Super-spiritual, if I need a well-documented excuse for being miserable. But what if I really want to change? Am I doomed for all time to be what I am; stuck forever with these nasty genes and learned patterns of behavior? "No!" declares the apostle Paul: "Therefore if any man be in Christ, he is a new creature: old things are passed away; behold, all things are become new" (II Cor. 5:17). As is so often true in spiritual growth, the thing that looks most difficult actually is the most simple . . . because God already has done it. *The Living Bible* paraphrases this verse: "When someone becomes a Christian he becomes a brand new person inside. He is not the same any more. A new life has begun."

You see, God knows that I cannot change my heredity. "Can the Ethiopian change the color of his skin? or a leopard take away his spots? Nor can you who are so used to doing evil now start being good" (Jer. 13:23 TLB). So God changes it *for* me. God becomes my Father. I am born again, a "joint-heir with Christ" to the kingdom of heaven.

The Starting Point

This is not a book on how to be born again. I suspect that most readers of this book know how to do that. (If you don't, read Billy Graham's excellent book by that name.) I *will* say though, that if any of you have *not* been born again (been saved, regenerated, justified by faith, or established a personal relationship with God through Christ) you cannot, according to Jesus, even *see* the kingdom of God.

You see, we do not become spiritual by doing spiritual things. We begin to do spiritual things because we *are* spiritual. You are a child of God. His Spirit lives in you. You are therefore declared to be righteous, free from sin, a holy saint, justified spiritually. It is a travesty of the gospel that most Christians try to become spiritual by doing—rather than doing spiritual things because of who they are.

125

A friend of mine, Julius Dodson, preaches it this way: "I ask people if they're saved and they say 'I hope so.' That's like asking me if I'm black and my saying, 'I hope so.' You either are black like me, or you aren't. In the same way, you either are saved, or you aren't." And if you are—you're spiritual. God says so.

Now lest you get all carried away, let me explain. I can just hear some of you saying, "Here we go again, easy believeism. I *was* saved and I'm *still* not very spiritual. I want an answer, and all I get is the same old stuff."

The problem is that spiritual people do not need to *act* spiritual. An old preacher used to say, "I got two dogs fighting in my middle. One wants me to do good, the other one wants me to do bad." When asked which one usually won, he replied, "Whichever one I say 'sic him' to."

Being born again is the essential first step in becoming like Christ. We cannot get there without it. But we might not get there *with* it, either. In C. S. Lewis' *Voyage of the Dawn Treader*, he comments on a boy who had had a born-again experience: "It would be nice, and fairly nearly true to say that 'from that time forth Eustace was a different boy.' To be strictly accurate, he *began* to be a different boy. He had relapses. There were still many days when he could be very tiresome. But most of those I shall not notice. The cure had begun."

We seem to become hung up at one extreme or the other between faith and works. Paul assures us that works cannot produce faith. James thunders back that faith without works is dead. Interestingly enough, *works* follows *faith* in the chronology of the New Testament. They need to be in that position also in our lives, if we are to be effective.

"For by grace are ye saved through faith; and that not of yourselves: it is the gift of God: Not of works, lest any man should boast. For we are his workmanship, created in Christ Jesus unto good works, which God hath before ordained that we should walk in them" (Eph. 2:8-10).

What Kind of Father?

Here I am primarily concerned not with *how* to acquire a new father, but with what *kind* of father to acquire. Most Christians I know are scared to death of God the Father. Not too long ago I talked with a couple who could not love each other. "Your problem," I asserted, "is that you can't give each other what you don't have. You don't see God loving you, so you in turn cannot love each other."

They were properly shocked. "Of course God loves us," they protested vehemently. "We've always been taught that, and we believe it." "So you do, in your heads," I agreed, "but not in your hearts." I then suggested an experiment to test their experience of God. You might try it, too.

Close your eyes and pretend that Jesus is taking you on a flight through space. Up you go, above the clouds, into the heavens. Fly with him, through dark vastness, past twinkling stars and lonely planets, to heaven itself. There on a great white throne sits God the Father. What kind of feelings do you have as he looks at you? The couple I was working with felt afraid and ashamed. They wanted to get away from God as fast as they could.

Was this couple Christian? Yes, these were two born-again, church-attending believers, who had many of the same feelings toward God that you do. And the travesty of it is that they learned those feelings from other Christians.

Fathers— Earthly and Heavenly

When you were very young, your parents were the only God you knew. They were huge, powerful, all-knowing, and made all the rules. I remember one night when I carried my three-year-old home from church. He looked up at the full moon in the bright summer sky and asked me what it was. "That's the moon, Matthew," I replied. "Get it for me, Daddy," he said, with full trust and faith in my omnipotence.

As you gradually came to realize that your parents were not all-powerful or as wise as you had thought, you began to transfer their Godlike qualities onto the real God. The problem is that you *also* transferred to God all their faults. If your parents were strict, mean, and tolerated no questioning of their rules, then your image of the Father probably is of a mean strict rulemaker who cannot be questioned.

What makes things worse is that parents, Sunday school teachers, and preachers often reinforce a child's poor image of God in order to make the child behave. "If you do that one more time, God will punish you," is a phrase that was heard often by children who, as adults, are now afraid of God. By threatening our youngsters with the wrath of the Almighty, we keep them docile, orderly, obedient tithe-payers who secretly hate God. Of course they would never admit this—even to themselves. So they super-spiritually pretend to love God totally and serve him willingly.

Love and Hate —For God?

In a recent therapy group, one of the members was trying an experiment in prayer. For once, she was going to throw away all her preconceived notions about what praying *should* be like and just tell God how she felt. For several minutes she poured out her fears, hatred, and disgust. She ended by sobbing, *"I hate you, God!* I hate you . . . and I love you, too."

Over the years, I have found that most people, especially evangelicals, need to experience their hate for God. We need to get into a rage and cry out, as Job and David did, that the life he gave us just is not fair! And as we experience our anger and frustration, we open ourselves, through honesty, to experience also his forgiveness and love.

What kind of Father is he? He is beyond our understanding. He does things his own way without my permission, and without even being so kind as to tell me what he's going to do. He never apologizes and he seldom explains. He runs the world effortlessly. In all this, he does not demand that I understand him, but that I love him unquestioningly.

He is good—but according to his own standards. His idea of *good* may not coincide with mine. He is love; yet his love may hurt me beyond measure. He invites me to share in his sufferings and thus to experience his joy. He is steadfast, unmovable, dependable. But as I follow him, my feet slip, and I become lost, and he seems so far away when I feel I need him.

At any rate, God is vastly different from my physical father. My earthly father loved me as well as he could; my heavenly Father loves me perfectly. God loves me constantly, whether or not I am good. He loves me wisely enough to do always what is good for me. His rules are always fair and his ways are always right. "The law of the Lord is perfect, converting the soul: the testimony of the Lord is sure, making wise the simple. . . . More to be desired are they than gold, yea, than much fine gold: sweeter also than honey and the honeycomb" (Ps. 19:7, 10).

He is sinless, pure, perfect—and he lives in *me!* I share a part of eternity as I share in his divine nature. We are one in worship, and I feel my heart strangely warmed as I cry out, "Abba, Father." I am his beloved son—and someday, Dad, I am going to be just like my Big Brother.

C H A P T E R   1 8

Changing My Environment

*Be careless in your dress if you must, but keep a tidy
soul.*   *—Mark Twain*

One of my parishioners, a computer specialist, tells me
that his computer is really one of the most stupid
"brains" in the company. "It really can't do anything by
itself, you know," he says. "It can do only what I tell it to
do." My friend says there is a formula which accounts for
most of his computer's mistakes. The formula is "garbage
in = garbage out."

Now that makes sense to me, as I think about
becoming spiritual. Just as my friend feeds wrong
information, or garbage, into the computer and gets
wrong answers from it, so I will get super-spiritualism
out of my soul if I feed garbage into it.

Getting Rid of the Garbage

Do not be deceived; God is not mocked, for whatever a man
sows, that he will also reap. For he who sows to his own flesh
will from the flesh reap corruption; but he who sows to the
Spirit will from the Spirit reap eternal life. And let us not grow

weary in well-doing, for in due season we shall reap, if we do not lose heart. (Galatians 6:7-9 RSV)

My wife and I have moved a lot in the past twenty years, and when we start to pack, I inevitably remark, "How did we ever accumulate all this stuff?" As I try to move farther and farther into God's spiritual plan for me, I wonder the same thing. How did I ever accumulate all this super-spiritual garbage that clutters up my life and chokes my spirit? The answer is that I sowed it myself, and now I am reaping the results.

Opening My Eyes

To continue Paul's analogy, how can I get rid of the corruption I am reaping and begin to sow for the Spirit? First of all, I need to pray that I will be able to see accurately. Remember the story of Elisha's servant (II Kings 6)? Elisha was camped near Dothan when the king of Syria sent a great army of chariots and horses to surround him.

When the prophet's servant woke up early the next morning, there were troops everywhere. "Alas, master, what shall we do now?" he cried out. "Don't be afraid," said Elisha. "Our army is bigger than theirs!" Then Elisha prayed, "Lord, open his eyes and let him see." And suddenly the young man saw what had been there all the time—the vast army of the Lord's angelic troops.

You and I need to see spiritual things if we are to sow for the Spirit. We need to ask God to show us what *he* thinks of the way we spend our money and our time. Look around your house. What pictures are hanging on your walls? What kind of music is in the air? What TV programs assault your soul? Examine your budget, your food, your schedule. Make a detailed list, so that you really will know how you spend your time and money.

131

Then begin to ask, "Lord, do you like this? What would you rather have me buy? How do you want me to spend my time? How can I change my environment to please you?" Remember that God is not interested in making you a martyr. He *is* interested in your happiness, which means long-term spiritual growth. Putting off the old person and putting on the new is usually troublesome— sometimes downright painful—but it is the only way to grow.

As I write these words, I brace myself for your inevitable onslaught. "Every book on spiritual growth, every sermon I've ever heard, has taught me that!" Yes, and just because I am repeating an old truth does not make it one bit less true. But many of those books and sermons not only instruct you to add to and subtract from your life—they define *what* to add and subtract.

I cannot define your additions and subtractions, for two reasons. First of all, I do not know what yours are. God wants to make you into a unique creature; therefore the things *he* adds and subtracts will be different from those anyone else would add and subtract. Second, even if I *did* know, I would not tell you. You need to learn to hear from *him*. If I told you, it would only spoil the delight and the pain of your discovery.

But What About . . .

Unfortunately, there are quite a few things in our environments that we cannot change. I live with five other people who do not usually want to change to suit me. I have a job that will not change, and our church likes to stay the same. Of course, I could change my job or my church if God wanted me to, but I am convinced that he does not. Now what? And what about my relatives, the weather, my country and its politics, my physical characteristics? Obviously, there are a lot of things we can do very little about.

What we *can* change is the way we look at those things. A group of psychologists thought they were writing something new when they said that people are not disturbed by reality, but by their *perception* of reality. In other words, you might not be angry with me, but if I *think* you are, it is just as bad. Eighteen hundred years ago, Epictetus said, "People are not upset by events, but by the view they take of the events."

You need to pray, "Lord, open my eyes and let me see." When you begin to look at the unchangeable from God's point of view, several things may happen. You may find that it is not so unchangeable after all. You almost certainly will find peace in your soul. You will begin to find the joy you thought you could not have, even if nothing changes—except *you.*

How did people see Jesus? Some merely saw him as a vaguely interesting preacher. Others, as a magician or a fraud. Some, as a danger to the social structure, and still others, as a possible political giant. Very few saw what God intended them to see. "There are none so blind as those who will not see." What do you see in your environment? What do you think God wants you to see?

For me, though, *seeing* what God wants me to see is not nearly as hard as *doing* what he wants me to do. If you have the same problem, let me give you this advice: Become accountable to someone.

You want to quit smoking? Join a support group. Tell your friends and family of your decision.

Do you feel you need to read the Scriptures and/or pray more? Become involved in a group that will hold you accountable to your commitment.

Do you want to change the way you react with your family? Make an appointment with your pastor or with a marriage counselor.

I find that when I make secret resolutions to change myself or my environment, the resolutions not only stay secret, they stay unchanged. When I receive the support (and nagging) of my family, friends, or groups I have joined, I change. I need to "confess my faults" to others, that I might be healed.

Sometimes when I commit myself to another person or to a group, a strange thing happens: I find that the thing I thought needed to be changed was all right in the first place! And sometimes I find that what I thought was all right is the very thing God wants me to change. This is called the ministry of the Body of Christ.

Do not super-spiritually pretend to know just how to change your environment (or anybody else's). Practice the Serenity Prayer used by Alcoholics Anonymous: "God grant me the serenity to accept the things I cannot change—the courage to change the things I can—and the wisdom to know the difference."

C H A P T E R 1 9

Changing My Choices

All she ever wanted out of life was one thing—her own way.
—Anonymous

All right, so I am now a new creation in Christ, according to the Bible. I have a new heredity and the Spirit of God dwells in me. Now all I need to do is change my environment (those parts I *can* change) and see things from God's point of view. The Bible says that I *can* do it. Then why don't I? *I do not WANT to!*

Ever since the Garden of Eden, the problem has been the same. We just do not want to do what God wants us to do.

"Pastor," said a nice woman recently, "I just don't think God forgives *willful* sin."

"Just what other kind of sin do you think there is?" I asked. The Lord described the Israelites to Moses as "a rebellious and stiff-necked people," and we are no different today.

It seems to me that there are two basic reasons for not wholeheartedly responding with joy to the commandments of God. First, we doubt that he is smart enough or loving enough to know what will make us happy. That is, we think that our goals and purposes in life are vastly different from his; that to surrender to his will is somehow to dedicate ourselves to missing all the excitement of life. Second, we doubt that he is concerned enough with us to give us good things, even if he wanted to.

I remember a saying that used to make the rounds at a certain Bible school: Don't ever pray for God's will for your life, or you will be sent to Africa! We have heard so many grizzly stories of heroic missionaries and martyrs that for some reason, we are led to believe that the will of God must be totally opposite from ours. When we have fun, therefore, we are vaguely guilty and afraid. It seems we dare not imagine that our Lord would approve of our having a good time.

We have forgotten the Old Testament descriptions of the feasts—the wine, the dancing, the song. We have forgotten that David danced before the Lord with all his might. We sin by neglecting the instruction to be "joyful in the Lord." We totally ignore the promise of Jesus that he will give us abundant life and joy that is full.

God Wants
—People Want

Some years ago, I took a survey to find out what our congregation thought people wanted out of life—what would make them happy. I have since repeated the survey many times with different groups, and it usually comes out the same each time. See if you agree.

Our survey reports that people desire money and financial security, good health, personal security in knowing that events are essentially predictable, and peace of mind and spirit. These four things I lump under the category *peace*.

People long for love and a sense of belonging; they want to know that someone cares. They spend great amounts of time and money on pleasure. They are very interested in sexual issues, and they want happy families. I classify these four things as *joy*.

The survey also indicates that most people want power in some form or other. They want esteem; they want others to admire and like them. They need a purpose for living, something sought for in philosophy and religion. And though it is not always apparent, moral goodness is also desperately desired by mankind. (If you do not believe this, listen to the justifications people come up with when confronted with their sin.) I call this last category *righteousness*.

Can I Have What I Want?— Can I Have What He Wants?

If you agree generally that these are the things most people want and strive for in life, the next question is obvious: Does God want us to have these things, or not? And if he does, why do we not have them? Is he punishing us? Are we not doing the right things or praying the right prayers? Is God unable to give us what he wants us to have?

Let me begin with the crucial question. Does God want the same things for me that I want for me? I believe the answer to be unquestionably and wholeheartedly *yes!* Here follows some scriptural evidence:

Money   I wish above all things that thou mayest prosper and be in health, even as thy soul prospereth (III John 1:2). Seek ye first the kingdom of God, and his righteousness; and all these things [clothing, food, etc.] shall be added unto you (Matt. 6:33).

Health   See III John 1:2 above. Bless the Lord, O my soul . . . who healeth all thy diseases (Ps. 103:2-3). If thou wilt diligently hearken to the voice of the Lord thy God . . . and keep all his statutes, I will put none of these

137

	diseases upon thee . . . for I am the Lord that healeth thee (Exod. 15:26).
Security	Jesus Christ the same yesterday, and to day and for ever (Heb. 13:8). My God shall supply all your need according to his riches in glory by Christ Jesus (Phil. 4:19).
Peace of Mind	Thou wilt keep him in perfect peace (Isa. 26:3). My peace I give unto you. . . . Let not your heart be troubled, neither let it be afraid (John 14:27).
Love	I have loved thee with an everlasting love (Jer. 31:3). I have loved you, saith the Lord (Mal. 1:2).
Pleasure	Thou shalt make them drink of the river of thy pleasure (Ps. 36:8). At thy right hand there are pleasures for evermore (Ps. 16:11).
Sex	Rejoice with the wife of thy youth. . . . Let her breasts satisfy thee at all times; and be thou ravished always with her love (Prov. 5:18-19). Let him kiss me with the kisses of his mouth: for thy love is better than wine (Song of Solomon 1:2).
Family	Whoso findeth a wife findeth a good thing (Prov. 18:22). Children are an heritage of the Lord. Happy is the man that hath his quiver full of them (Ps. 127:3, 5).
Power	Ye shall receive power, after that the Holy Ghost is come upon you (Acts 1:8). The God of Israel is he that giveth strength and power unto his people (Ps. 68:35).
Esteem	Let us make man in our image (Gen. 1:26). Thou hast made him a little lower than the angels, and hast crowned him with glory and honour (Ps. 8:5).

Purpose	As my Father hath sent me, even so send I you (John 20:21). Thou madest him to have dominion over the works of thy hands; thou hast put all things under his feet (Ps. 8:6).
Moral Goodness	Now ye are clean through the word which I have spoken unto you (John 15:3). There is therefore now no condemnation to them which are in Christ Jesus. For the law of the Spirit of life in Christ Jesus hath made me free from the law of sin and death (Rom. 8:1, 2).

So God actually wants the same things for me that *I* want for me. If that is true, why do I not have them? Is it because he is unable to give them to me? Hardly! "Thine, O Lord, is the greatness, and the power, and the glory, and the victory, and the majesty: . . . in thine hand is power and might; and in thine hand it is to make great, and to give strength unto all" (I Chron. 29:11-12).

If the problem is not with God, it must be with me. Somehow, I am not responding correctly to the good hand of God. He has written the check, but I seem unable to cash it. Romans 14:17 will give us a clue: "The kingdom of God is not meat and drink; but *righteousness*, and *peace*, and *joy* in the Holy Ghost" (italics added). Remember those three words? If you agree with me that they sum up all that humankind wants, and all that God wants us to have, we have the answer to our dilemma.

What Is a Kingdom?

Most people translate *kingdom of God* to mean *heaven*. I disagree. A kingdom is anywhere a king rules. Heaven is the *ultimate* expression of the kingdom of God, but my heart is its *immediate* concern. "The kingdom of God is at hand; repent" (Mark 1:15 RSV), urged Jesus. In other words, let God rule your minds and hearts and you will have everything you want and need! "They that seek the Lord," declared the psalmist, "shall not want *any* good thing" (Ps. 34:10, italics added).

But God has his own way to bring me this righteousness, peace, and joy . . . and it is nothing like *my* way, even though both God and I desire the same results. Bill Gothard is fond of saying that if he wants to know how God will work, he just thinks, "How would *I* do that" . . . and *God's* way is usually just the opposite. "There is a way which seemeth right unto a man, but the end thereof are the ways of death" (Prov. 14:12).

Jesus' ways for me to obtain what both God and I want me to have are unusual, to say the least. In fact, they are downright radical! They are found in Matthew, chapters four through seven—otherwise known as the Sermon on the Mount. This mind-blowing prescription for finding happiness includes such strange things as loving my enemies, forgiving everybody who has hurt me, and returning good for evil. We do not operate like that. But God does.

Who's in Charge Here?

The question, then, is not How can I do it? or What does God want me to do? but rather, Will I do what I know God wants me to do? "Everybody is going around trying to get a new revelation, a new message from God," says my friend Ward Williams, "when they aren't *doing* one quarter of the things they already *know!*" God has chosen to live in me. That means that I can do anything he wants me to do.

The power is there; the "want to" is not. But, to quote Dr. Williams again, "The price of spiritual progress is obedience to the known will of God." *You* are not responsible for the power—God is. *You* are not responsible for the knowledge—God is. *Your* responsibility is to *do* what you *know*. . . . It is hard, for we are by nature stubborn, stiff-necked, and rebellious. But remember, in the end, God wants the same things we want.

One last thing. God's choices for you will be especially designed for you. He knows that each of us needs different amounts of the good things in life. For instance, esteem and purpose are more important to me than pleasure and security. God will design a program of choices for me that is tailor-made to suit his purpose for my life.

Don't be upset, then, if your program of choices is utterly different from that of others around you. It is *supposed* to be. But, of course, you *could* be super-spiritual and copy theirs.

C H A P T E R 2 0

Who's a Hypocrite?

Waiting for Super-Spiritual Feelings

Hypocrite reader—my fellow man—my brother!
—*Charles Baudelaire*

She sat in the chair like a crouched lion, and I was beginning to feel like the prey. Her eyes narrowed in obvious rage; her body was held taut; her voice had an angry edge. And yet at the same time, she seemed pleased with herself.

"Well, I followed your advice, John," she spit out. "I tried to just be myself. And now nobody likes me. It was better when I was a hypocrite. At least then they left me alone. Now everybody wants to know what's *wrong* with me."

"Wait a minute, Carol," I countered. "What did you actually *do* that everyone is so upset about?"

"Well," she answered slowly, "I didn't want to be a hypocrite anymore. So when I felt like doing something, I just did it; if I didn't feel like doing it, I didn't do it. Isn't that what you told me to do?"

As we continued the session, I discovered that Carol had told off her husband and mother-in-law, ignored her housework, and stayed home from church, among other things, because she "just didn't feel like it and didn't want to be hypocritical about it." What was wrong? She had fallen prey to yet another super-spiritual trap—the it's-OK-to-do-anything-I-want-as-long-as-I'm-not-phony-about-it syndrome.

Doing Your Own Thing

There are a lot of books on the market today that advise you to do your own thing at any price: Win by intimidating your opponent; be yourself, no matter who it hurts; no one can tell you how to live your life, and so on, and so on. As I reflect upon the last several chapters, it strikes me that this could well become another such book. I hope not.

A short time ago, I was a guest on a local talk show. The topic was Attitudes Toward Premarital Sex, and the discussion was lively. One young girl, who wanted her parents' approval of her relationship with her boyfriend, was enthusiastically making the point that "our sexuality has always been open and honest; why do they get so uptight?" Another guest got right to the point: "I think you're confusing honesty with righteousness. Just because you sin openly and honestly doesn't make it any less a sin."

I remember a comic strip in which a certain character was drinking, shooting at "the revenooers," gambling, and fighting. When asked, "What're ye doin', Paw?" he responded, "*My thing!*" It is not the purpose of this book to encourage you to do your *own* thing. Its purpose is to persuade you to do *God's thing* for *you*, which will be different from God's thing for anyone else. The danger, though, is that you, like Carol, may react so strongly against years of manipulation by friends, family, and church that you will swing too far in the other direction.

Erma Bombeck, in a spoof on self-help books, has this to report:

I had finally learned how to be a good friend to myself. When I thought about it, I was my ONLY friend. I took me everywhere; to the movies, the zoo, long rides in the country. I dined with me over intimate dinners and turned my head with flowers and candy. I knew I was getting too involved with me, but I couldn't seem to stop myself. We got along wonderfully. I knew when to talk to me and when to shut up. I knew when I was in a bad mood and when I wanted to be alone with just me.

I praised me when I did a good job and spoiled me outrageously. There wasn't anything I could deny myself because I was such a wonderful person. If anyone had a snout-ful of self-esteem it was me. People were beginning to talk, spread rumors about my extramarital affair with myself, but I didn't care. What I felt for me was genuine. (I think I even told me that I wanted to have a baby.) . . . I stood in front of a mirror and said "I love you," to which my husband would always yell, "You say that now, but will you respect you in the morning?" . . .

I looked in the mirror at my best friend for the past few months and waited for her to say something. The truth hit me. I didn't love me very much.

During the past year I have come to grips with midlife, found inner peace, fought outer life, interpreted my fantasies, examined my motives for buying, dissected my marriage, charted my astrological stars and become my best AND ONLY friend. I have brought order to my life, meditated, given up guilt, adjusted to the new morality, and spent every living hour understanding me, interpreting me and loving me—and you know what? I'm bored to death with me. If I never hear another word about me it will be too soon. *(Aunt Erma's Cope Book)*

Many of those whom I counsel go through a period I call Adolescence II. They come in originally with depression, poor self-esteem, shyness, and physical symptoms. Gradually, as they come to realize their super-spiritual games, those symptoms begin to diminish and are replaced with anger and rage.

The formerly super-spiritually meek and mild turn with a vengeance upon parents, spouse, church, and any other object or person that they perceive (sometimes quite correctly) has helped to keep them in their self-defeating games. I often receive phone calls from spouses at this point. "If this is what counseling does to people, it ought to be outlawed! My Carol used to be easy to get along with, but you've turned her into a monster!" Usually, if the spouse will just be patient, my counselee will grow *through* this stage of rebellion and rage into another stage—that of real love. That is, unless he or she falls into another trap:

Super-Spiritual Antihypocrisy

Perhaps we should examine *hypocrisy;* then I can explain the super-spiritual trap. Of all sins, Jesus seems to be more upset about hypocrisy than any other. Observe the way he forgives the woman caught in adultery: "Neither do I condemn thee, go and sin no more." Be with him as he associates with "sinners and publicans." Watch him beside the well in Samaria as he ministers to a woman who has had five husbands. Then notice the contrast as he rebukes the Pharisees.

"Woe to you, Pharisees, and you other religious leaders. Hypocrites! For you won't let others enter the Kingdom of Heaven, and won't go in yourselves. And you pretend to be holy" (Matt. 23:13-14 TLB). Jesus continues his tongue lashing: "You hypocrites! You are like whitewashed tombs, which look fine on the outside but are full of bones and decaying corpses on the inside. You snakes and sons of snakes! How do you expect to escape from being condemned to hell?" (27, 33 TEV).

These words are really amazing when we consider that the Pharisees were the *good* guys. It was the Sadducees and the Herodians who were selling out their religious heritage for Roman protection. The Essenes were first-century dropouts, and the Zealots were an ancient form of our modern-day terrorists. The Pharisees, on the other hand, worked with the people, encouraging righteousness, charity to the poor, and piety toward

145

God. To accomplish these worthwhile ends, they encouraged strict obedience to the letter of the law.

There was a superstitious belief among the Pharisees that if every Jew would observe all the laws of Moses (as interpreted by the Pharisees) for one day, the Messiah would appear. They would study, teach, and argue with one another, day and night, about the meaning of this or that law. They worried, exhorted, observed, and fretted about points which seem to us preposterous nonsense. And so they seemed also to Jesus. "You people would strain at a gnat and swallow a camel."

What Is Hypocrisy?

Yet it was not their nit-picking that angered our Lord; that merely amused him. It was their obvious attempt to pretend on the outside the spirituality that did not exist on the inside that inspired his wrath: "How terrible for you . . . Pharisees! You hypocrites! You clean the outside of your cup and plate, while the inside is full of what you have gotten by violence and selfishness. Blind Pharisee! Clean what is inside the cup first, and the outside will be clean too! . . . On the outside you appear good to everybody, but inside you are full of hypocrisy and sins" (Matt. 23:25-28 TEV).

There is that word again—*hypocrisy*. What does it mean to be a hypocrite? Am I one? And if so, what can I *do* about it? Webster defines *hypocrisy* as *the act of playing a part on a stage, a pretending to be what one is not*. *Roget's Thesaurus* compares the word with other words: *deception, falseness, fraud, deceit, mask,* and *camouflage*. Hypocrisy is the core of all super-spiritualism; it springs from our being more concerned with *appearing* good than with *becoming* good through repentance.

But if that is what hypocrisy *is*, this is what it is *not*—doing the right thing even though I do not want to do it. It is *not* OK to do anything I want as long as I am not phony about it! Similarly, it is *not* hypocritical to do the right thing, the loving thing, even when I do *not* want to do it. In fact, it is very spiritual to *do* a righteous act without righteous feelings. But it is *super-spiritual* to pretend that I want to do it when I do *not* want to do it.

If I waited for good feelings to motivate me, I would never finish this book! I would treat my family and friends unfairly. I rarely even would get out of bed, because I almost never *want* to get out of bed in the morning. Love and righteousness are acts of the *will* and can be performed whenever I *choose*, whether I enjoy performing them or not.

"Love your enemies," says Jesus. "Pray for those who persecute you" (Matt. 5:44 RSV). Do good things for those who hate you. Make peace with your brother. Stop judging your friends and seek first the kingdom of God (see Matt. 5:46-48, 23-25; 7:7; 6:33). Nowhere does he say that I need to *feel* loving, good, peaceful, or in any way spiritual. He says I need to *act* spiritual.

But the problem is this: Whenever I try to do what Christ teaches, I begin to collect the applause of my family, friends, and worse yet, myself. I actually begin to believe that there is something in me, other than the love of Christ, which is good. Paul knew better. "I know I am rotten through and through" (Rom. 7:18 TLB).

"The world consists almost exclusively of people who are like one sort and who behave like another sort," says Zona Gale. But do they pretend that they really *are* another sort? That would be super-spiritual. If they cheerfully admit their sinful feelings and desires and decide to act righteously anyway, that is spiritual. Nowhere in Scripture do I read that Jesus enjoyed dying on the cross for me. I read that he set his face "like a flint" towards Jerusalem and *decided* to die for me.

Do not wait for loving feelings. You will *not* be a hypocrite if you do loving things for God, your family, and yourself. You will be a Christian! You will be spiritual.

CHAPTER 21

Your Basic Spiritual Church

Unto him be glory in the church. —*Ephesians 3:21*

On Sunday mornings not long ago, in a small rented room at the Downriver YMCA, met your basic spiritual church. Christ Church of Downriver is small, young (I am the oldest, at 39), charismatic, and a bit on the intellectual side. We dress in casual clothing, like the sound of guitars, and really enjoy having meals together. None of the above makes us spiritual. Now we meet in rented space at Southgate Community Church, and that has not made us spiritual, either.

We meet in small groups in our homes to discuss spiritual gifts, C. S. Lewis' Narnia books, and the way the Bible relates to marriage. Our women's softball team took first place last year. We have a constitution and bylaws. We like to use the New International Version of the Bible. None of those things sound very spiritual. So why do I claim spirituality for this church?

First of all, the majority of the people present at any service are there because they *want* to be there. This is due mostly to the fact that our church is less than five years old. There is no great force of habit, no pastoral guilt trip compelling anyone to come to Christ Church. I

148

work full time at a Christian counseling center, and I have neither the time nor the inclination to badger people who miss church. This usually results in a small but very enthusiastic crowd. We have come to worship, not to fulfill an obligation.

Second, we are committed to personal and corporate growth in Christ. Since most other churches are, too, perhaps it would be a good idea to spell out what this means to us. The apostle Peter gave us the following steps: "Add to your faith goodness; and to goodness, knowledge; and to knowledge, self-control; and to self-control, perseverance; and to perseverence, godliness; and to godliness, brotherly kindness; and to brotherly kindness, love" (II Pet. 1:5-7 NIV).

Peter claimed that if we follow this pattern we will share in God's nature, escape worldly corruption, become effective and productive in our ministry, never fall out of grace, and receive an abundant entrance into heaven. Sounds good to me!

We are growing, then, as a Body and as separate parts of it, in three areas: intellectual knowledge, emotional stability and depth, and behavioral conduct. The highest expression of this growth will be love—the love of God and of our neighbors. So far, so good. Very few churches will disagree with this. So here is our third principle: We expect that each member's growth will be unique.

My Growth = Your Growth?

This means that you and I most surely will grow differently. We most likely will grow in different areas, in different directions, and at different speeds. My rules of conduct will probably be a bit different from your rules. My theology will be different in some areas from yours. You and I will think, feel, and behave differently about some issues.

Now, this is true in any church. Our difference is that

149

not only do we expect these differences—we actually encourage them!

When people grow in this manner, one of the by-products is confusion. Another is disagreement. This can be devastating to a church which insists that its people should not disagree and that confusion is a bad thing. (I know that in I Cor. 14:33, Paul says that God is not the author of confusion; but he was talking about regulating the meeting of the church, not about the way people grow.)

Confusion and disagreement are necessary evils if we are to change. Do you remember when you first tried to comprehend higher math, logic, or a foreign language? It was necessary to get through and resolve the stage of confusion and disagreement before you could reach understanding. So since God's ways are not our ways, and his thoughts are not our thoughts, be prepared to be thoroughly confused as you search them out for your life. Be prepared also to have your brother disagree with your conclusions.

In Christ Church, we have a motto—Always Disagree Agreeably. This motto applies to our Bible study, our marriages, and our annual church meetings. We do not always accomplish this goal, but its very existence stops a lot of bitterness before it starts.

Honesty Is the Best Policy

Fourth, Christ Church is more interested in what the members really think than in whether they toe the party line. They are encouraged to speak up, both privately and publicly, on issues that concern them. On Sunday nights, we open up the discussion of a specific topic so that everyone can have a chance to speak. We sometimes break up into groups of three or four so that each person *must* speak. How can we minister to people if we do not know what they think or what they need?

Now, do not misunderstand me; we have our belief system. We have a constitution and bylaws that spell out our doctrine of God, Scripture, baptism, salvation, spiritual gifts, and church government (and a lot more). Members are expected to hold to these beliefs and to terminate membership if they seriously depart from them. But members who are growing must, from time to time, challenge, question, and confront these issues in their growth. Thus the statement "I don't know if I believe this anymore" is expected and dealt with lovingly and seriously, rather than with shock or smugness. It is not unspiritual to doubt—it is super-spiritual to pretend that you do not doubt.

Sour Fruit?

Jesus said that we could judge a tree by its fruit. So what kind of spiritual fruit (Gal. 5:22) have these four principles produced? First, our people love one another. Not too well, sometimes, but they do love one another. They are involved with one another, they care about one another. They call each other on the phone when they have problems. They help each other when help is needed. When they say, "I missed you last week," *they mean it!*

Second, our church functions are characterized by joy. We really have a lot of fun together. Whether they are playing softball, singing hymns, or reading the Bible, the people in our church enjoy themselves. They are often heard to say that their vacations were fun, but that they really missed being in church. We went out to dinner at a Greek restaurant not long ago. Ours were the only tables that had no wine, and I know we made more noise than any of the people who were drinking!

Third, we are basically at peace with one another. Oh, we have had our problems, but our official meetings are almost boring, they are so peaceful. Because we encourage honesty, problems are solved, and people get rid of their anger before it turns to bitterness. Our ball team won an award for sportsmanship last year. The elders spend more time in Bible study and prayer than in arguing about business. This kind of fruit leads me to believe that Christ Church is on the right track.

In short, we let one another be what we are instead of trying to make everybody be what we think they *should* be. The people don't always understand me or agree with me. But they love me. They enjoy me. I love and enjoy them; and we are at peace with one another. I think that's pretty spiritual.

Good Heavens!

It occurs to me, as I review this last chapter, that I have described an almost perfect church. Nothing could be further from the truth. We become angry at one another, misunderstand and misuse one another. We are guilty of every sin imaginable. How could it be otherwise? —unless, of course, we were super-spiritual.

C H A P T E R   2 2

What Do I Do Now?

Some Practical Ways to Grow Spiritually

Whether this book lives or not is not so important to me now as my search for something new to say and share in the next one.   —David Viscott

Call it my neurotic need for closure, or my Red Cross complex, but I would feel incomplete if I neglected to give you *something* practical, something you can *do*, for heaven's sake! So many books point up the problem beautifully, but leave you hanging. This is because, being sinners, we authors know how to write about sin. Being super-spiritual at heart, I write very well about super-spirituality.

Let me give you four ways to grow that I have found helpful. Some will fit you nicely, and some will not. Let me plead with you to try the ones that do *not* fit—especially those that hurt or those that are frightening. I have found that nothing hurts or helps more than a wound that cuts through the illusion and makes us see through ourselves.

Grow Through Passive Input

First and probably easiest, begin to expand your mind through *passive input*. Passive input consists of anything you can put into yourself without outwardly reacting toward it. Books, lectures, and television fall into this category.

Every two weeks or so, the Sterner family makes a pilgrimage to the local library. We carry in one box full of books and carry out another. (Not watching much TV gives us more time to read.) We also buy books, used and new; swap books; and borrow books. What do we read? Anything! Everything! Here are a few of our picks.

Book Suggestions from John

To expand your mind, read anything by C. S. Lewis. Francis Schaeffer writes some heavy philosophy. Try Basilea Schlink, Walter Trobish, Catherine Marshall, and Hannah Hurnard. *Mr. God, This Is Anna* by Flynn should loosen some cobwebs; also, *The Velveteen Rabbit* (a children's story?) by Margery Williams. Try subscribing to a magazine published by a denomination or an organization with a viewpoint opposite from yours—especially if it attacks your camp.

You want to laugh at yourself? Read anything by Erma Bombeck, Jean Kerr, or Shel Silverstein (especially *The Giving Tree* by Silverstein). Try *It's Hard to Be Hip Over Thirty* by Judith Viorst and *A Bag of Noodles* by Wally Armbruster.

Is understanding yourself or your mate what you want? Try the books by those names written by Cecil Osborne. Read anything by Charlie Shedd, Keith Miller, or Bruce Larson. Read *Born to Win* and *Born to Love* by James and Jongeward. Try *Healing Love* and *Man the Manipulator* by Everett Shostrum. *Your Inner Child of the Past* by Hugh Missildine and *Guilt and Freedom* by Bruce Narramore are excellent. Almost anything by Norman Wright or Gary Collins will be very helpful. By the way, when was the last time you read the Bible through?

Book Suggestions from Cheryl (John's wife)

Any book by George Macdonald, Elisabeth Elliot, or Hannah Hurnard is a good choice. *The Little Prince* by

Antoine de Saint-Exupery, *Streams in the Desert* by Mrs. Charles E. Cowan, and the poetry of Francis J. Roberts all are high on my list.

My favorite books on family living are by Joseph and Lois Bird and Dr. James Dobson. *No Fault Marriage* by Marcia Lasswell, *Liberated Parents, Liberated Children* by Faber and Mazlish, *Creative Counterpart* by Linda Dillow, and *The Secret of Married Love* by Anna Mow are all terrific.

Other favorite books are *Watership Down* by Richard Adams, *Blessings* by Mary Craig, and *Food for God's Children* by Raphael Gasson. Good books on sex are *Celebration in the Bedroom* by Charlie Shedd, *The Act of Marriage* by Tim and Beverly LaHaye, and especially *Solomon on Sex* by Joseph Dillow.

Books for the Kids

Though the teens like magazines best *(Seventeen, Campus Life, Mad)*, the Sterner kids also like the following: *The Tales of Narnia* (best of all, and liked by John and Cheryl, too) by C. S. Lewis, *Charlie and the Chocolate Factory* by Roald Dahl, the Oz series by L. Frank Baum, and the George and Martha books by Marshall (John loves anything by Marshall). Joseph P. Blank's *19 Steps Up the Mountain* is one of Joy's favorites (no one told her it was for adults), and the whole family likes *World* magazine, published by the National Geographic Society.

Other Passive Input

Besides reading (which most of you already do—I mean you *did* get *this* far, didn't you?), there are various other forms of passive input that will stimulate your mind, *if you let them!* Go to a good movie (I know there are not many, but look for one). I cried for three solid hours as I identified with Tevye in *Fiddler on the Roof*.

Go to your local community theater, attend a lecture series, buy some tapes of outstanding sermons. You could even go as far as to (gasp!) selectively watch certain TV programs. The important thing is that you keep consistently in mind the question, What does God want to show me through this experience; how can I use it for spiritual growth?

Reach Out to Others

The second way people grow is through *relationships*. When I bounce my ideas, feelings, and experiences off other persons and hear their reactions, it helps me to clarify my own position and provides me with another, perhaps more objective viewpoint. And also, when I feel that I am important enough to be heard by another, I feel loved, and my self-esteem goes up.

Try a Group

Where do we find these relationships? I hope you can find them through a church. Some churches are providing counseling services, support groups, small Bible study or prayer groups. The content focus of the group is less important than whether one can say what one needs to say without fear of being put down. The Lifestyle adult Sunday school materials put out by David C. Cook Publishing Company, the materials from Serendipity House and Abingdon, and the Creative Resources of Word, Incorporated, are designed to help local churches provide this kind of group.

If your church does not have this kind of group, why not ask your pastor about starting one? A discussion of this book might be a way to shake up a few dry bones. If you cannot motivate your church, ask around to find out where such a group meets. Then *join it,* for heaven's sake! Don't worry about being new or being accepted; if they do not accept you, it is not the right kind of group.

Find a Friend

Where can we find someone who will rejoice when we rejoice and weep when we weep? Is the song right, when it asserts that there is no friend like Jesus, "no not one"? I believe that our congregations are full of people who would like to care and be cared about, but who are too afraid to take the first step. *You* can take that step!

Invite someone over for coffee. Ask somebody to be your prayer partner (then dare to give them something real to pray about). Tell your pastor that you have read this book and that you want to meet periodically to review your spiritual growth. Ask for a plan designed specifically for you.

Do You Need a Shrink?

What about professional counseling? Since I do that for a living, you might expect me to encourage all those who wonder whether they need therapy to seek it. Well, I *do!* Go to a reputable therapist, by all means, if you think you might benefit from it. Have your pastor recommend one. Tell the therapist right off that the first thing you want to know is whether or not you need therapy—and why. If the therapist cannot give you any good reason why you need it, forget it!

I have grown through therapy—both individual and group—several times. Do not be ashamed to go for help when you need it. If your pastor cannot give you the name of a good therapist, write to the Christian Association for Psychological Studies, 26705 Farmington Road, Farmington Hills, Michigan 48018. They have a list of Christian therapists in most communities.

*Be Like Your Maker—
Make Something*

A third way to grow is by *being creative!* It is my opinion that one of the ways I share in the image of God is through my instinct for creativity. Write something— anything! Writing forces us to organize our thoughts in some logical manner. Take a creative writing class at your local college. Start a diary. Write a poem. Write a letter to God and tell him how hard it is to grow. Make a prayer list. Write!

Draw, paint, or sculpt something. It does not need to be "good" and you do not need to show it to anybody. Get into ceramics, china painting, or macrame. Learn to play an instrument, garden, dance, become involved with a theater group. Make bird houses, throw pottery, melt candles, or decorate cakes, but for the Creator's sake and your own, create something!

Do Something for Somebody

Fourth, *become involved in ministry*. But expand your conception of the meaning of *ministry*. Do something for somebody. Contact your Red Cross or other community agencies. Answer the phone for your church. Go visit some shut-ins. Join the choir or put out the bulletin. Walk in a walk-a-thon or collect for a charity. Give someone a cup of cold water in the name of Christ.

Those are my four ways to grow—now think of four of your own. Do not be limited by this book. "Grow in Christ" is not a suggestion; it is an *order*. But it does not need to be a drag. Growing can be fun, boring, painful, surprising, or all of the above. Moreover, it is our destiny. It is absolutely demanded by God. It is the only thing that, in the end, satisfies.

Let me close this book with my very favorite quotation—from *The Velveteen Rabbit* by Margery Williams:

"What is *real?*" asked the Rabbit one day, when they were lying side by side near the nursery fender, before Nana came to tidy the room. "Does it mean having things that buzz inside you and a stick-out handle?"

"Real isn't how you are made," said the Skin Horse. "It's a

thing that happens to you. When a child loves you for a long, long time, not just to play with, but *really* loves you, then you become real."

"Does it hurt?" asked the Rabbit. "Sometimes," said the Skin Horse, for he was always truthful. "When you are Real you don't mind being hurt."

"Does it happen all at once, like being wound up," he asked, "or bit by bit?"

"It doesn't happen all at once," said the Skin Horse. "You become. That's why it doesn't often happen to people who break easily, or have sharp edges, or who have to be carefully kept. Generally, by the time you are Real, most of your hair has been loved off, and you get loose in the joints and very shabby. But these things don't matter at all, because once you are Real you can't be ugly, except to people who don't understand."

So grow! In spite of your past, your family and friends— even in spite of the church. Become your own unique self. Be *real!* Anything else would be super-spiritual.

John Sterner is a pastor, psychotherapist, and marriage counselor in the Detroit area, where he lives with his wife Cheryl and their four children. He is a popular speaker on marriage and family topics and is chairman of the board of Challenge House, an in-patient drug-abuse center. A graduate of the University of Michigan and Central Michigan University, he is working on his doctorate in clinical psychology at Fielding Institute in Santa Barbara, California. His address is 2454 4th Street, Trenton, Michigan 48183 (telephone 313–563-4142), and he would be happy to hear from readers of this book.